Canada and the
French-Canadian Question

In nine brilliantly informed essays, Ramsay
Cook analyses the great Canadian problem.
He discusses the original meaning of Confederation and indicates the recent changes.
Without losing sight of the emotion that
shaped such issues as the Riel Rebellion and
the Ontario and Manitoba school questions,
he places them accurately in history and
politics. The author's knowledge of Quebec
is so sure that he has regularly written in
Le Devoir and in the influential *Cité libre*.
His articles have particular significance today, when Quebec students may go straight
from a lecture to a protest march.

RAMSAY COOK was born in 1931 in Ala-
meda, Saskatchewan, and educated at the
University of Manitoba, Queen's University,
and the University of Toronto. He is now
Associate Professor of History, University
of Toronto.

Canada and the French-Canadian Question

RAMSAY COOK

1967 / MACMILLAN OF CANADA / TORONTO

Reprinted 1967

Printed in Canada by Hignell Printing Limited

To the Memory of Professor J. H. S. Reid

Acknowledgments

Although some modifications have been made in the essays as they appear in this volume, all but two have appeared in print before. The exceptions are 'The Meaning of Confederation', which is a lecture delivered at the University of Vermont in April 1965, and 'Quebec, Ontario, and the Nation', which was prepared for a conference of Quebec and Ontario newspapermen held in Toronto in October 1965. One essay was first prepared for the Canadian Broadcasting Corporation's 'University of the Air' in May 1964; another was presented to a seminar at Dartmouth College in November 1964; a third began life as a lecture at McGill University in February 1964. 'Quebec: The Ideology of Survival' appeared, in a slightly altered form, in *The Prospect of Change* edited by Abraham Rotstein and published by McGraw-Hill. I would like therefore to thank these institutions and also the following publications for permission to use this material again: *Canadian Forum, Cité libre, International Journal, Tamarack Review, Queen's Quarterly*, the Montreal *Star*, and the *Political Quarterly*.

Several people helped in the publication of this book, and I would like to record my gratitude to them. Jim Bacque of Macmillan encouraged me to bring these essays together, and supervised the birth of the book. Pierre-Elliott Trudeau, who has taught me a great deal about both French Canada and nationalism, read and criticized two of the essays. Mr. George Ferguson of the Montreal *Star* and M. Claude Ryan of *Le Devoir* provided me with opportunities to put my ideas before Quebec audiences. Naturally the most valuable help in writing these essays was given to me by my wife, Eleanor. The faults in the final product are, of course, my own.

RAMSAY COOK

Contents

Canada and the
French-Canadian Question

Introduction

One of the articles of an historian's faith is that people would find the present less mysterious if they had a fuller understanding of the past. It was largely in this belief that the present collection of essays was written. It has always seemed to me that the difficulties between French- and English-speaking Canadians would be less bewildering if each partner knew a little more of the other's history. I would not be so bold as to suggest that the problems could be solved if we understood our history better. I merely say that the problems would be more easily identified.

The importance of understanding the background to our problems is fairly obvious. It is not that an understanding of the past will automatically supply panaceas for present or future problems. If that were so, historians would be statesmen, and that, alas, is rarely true. Instead, a little historical understanding may remove problems from the realm of mystery to the realm where rational solutions may be sought. Much of the irrationality apparent in the discussion of the relations between French and English Canadians in the past few years obviously stems from a lack of knowledge about our common history.

Each of the essays in this book approaches either the

French-Canadian question or the Canadian question from a particular angle. Some are almost wholly historical while others represent an attempt to analyse aspects of contemporary history. Although some deal with French Canada alone, and others relate to French-English relations, I do not see these as separate questions. Canada and the French-Canadian question is really the Canadian question.

A large number of people who are historically and juridically Canadians, but whose roots are found in French culture, are dissatisfied with the country's present organization. Essentially they are dissatisfied with the place of their culture in Canada, though their grievances are manifested in political, economic, and constitutional terms. If nearly a third of the people of Canada were discontented because they lacked employment or food or proper medical services, a Canadian problem of the first magnitude would almost immediately be recognized to exist. A substantial number of Canadians are dissatisfied with their status in Confederation. Unless this condition is clearly recognized as the primary Canadian problem, then there is a considerable possibility that French Canadians may decide that it is an exclusively French-Canadian problem. It is this essentially Canadian problem that is examined in the essays in this book.

Historians are more often asked questions about the present and the future than they are about the past, which is what they are supposed to know something about. While I have no more certain knowledge about the future than the next man, my reading of the history of Canada suggests that there are some steps that might be taken, and some attitudes that might be adopted, which would go a little distance towards restoring the equilibrium in French-English relations. There are in the essays that follow some explicit and implicit suggestions. They make no claim to great originality, as a summary will show.

First, I think we must find institutions that will give full expression to the cultural duality of the Canadian nation-state. Some are obvious. French-language education must be provided where there are enough French-speaking Canadians to make it practical. These institutions should be designed to meet the needs of French Canadians who live outside Quebec, but they would also increase the mobility of Quebeckers, who are at present reluctant to leave their province because of the lack of educational facilities in French for their children. The federal government must continue the process of transforming itself into an institution that will serve French- and English-speaking Canadians equally well.

Second, it should be obvious from the essays which follow that I am unconvinced by any argument so far presented of the necessity of rewriting our constitution. On the other hand, it is quite possible that amendments may be necessary. What is important, it seems to me, is that English Canadians show a willingness to examine sympathetically and with care every *specific* proposal for change that is advanced. French Canadians, and others who advocate constitutional change, must accept, on their part, the necessity of advancing *specific* proposals. Constitutions are not constructed out of generalities.

Finally, English Canadians must not allow themselves to be frightened by bogeys. Quebec is not and never has been a province exactly the same as the others, culturally or constitutionally. In fact, of course, very few of the provinces are exactly like the others. As long as the essential federal structure of the constitution is retained, there is no reason to cry doom and destruction if Quebec, or some other province, is treated differently in some respects or follows policies different from the other provinces. Administrative devices can frequently be found which satisfy the needs of both national standards and provincial and regional peculiarities. That is the main virtue of federalism. One principle of our federal system which should not be sacrificed is that of equalization: no Canadian should be penalized simply because he lives in a section of the country that has fewer economic advantages than the rich sections.

Above all, it is the thesis of these essays that there is no solution to our problems in the conjuring up of some new formula for a Canadian nationalism. That has always been the recommended policy in the past, a fact which in itself suggests that it is ill conceived. My view is that we have had too much, not too little, nationalism in Canada, and that our various nationalisms are the chief threat to the peace and survival of Canada. Today, French and English Canadians are moving towards an impasse because each is swayed by outdated concepts of nationalism, Canadian and French-Canadian. What is necessary is rational and pragmatic solutions designed to meet the needs of human beings; nationalism is an emotion which hides real problems behind an abstraction.

No Canadian was more aware of the dangers of nationalist appeals in politics than Henri Bourassa, though he did not always avoid such appeals himself. In 1902 he wrote:

It is to the racial instinct that politicians appeal in order to blind us when they are forced to choose between duty and power. It is the same instinct that is addressed when one wishes to force the people to give their confidence to certain men among them even when they have betrayed the national interest or dishonoured the position that they occupy through corruption, debauchery, and malversation of all sorts. In a word, it is by speculating on this instinct that one seeks to draw from us a guilty indulgence for the rene-

of uneasiness about the country's direction and future remains widespread. Bruce Hutchison, a veteran journalist and staunch Canadian nationalist, observed recently that Lester Pearson is the first prime minister 'who can no longer be sure' that Canadians are willing to continue to pay the price of nationhood. While there is continuing concern about Canada's unequal partnership with the United States, the major source of the country's present difficulties is domestic, not foreign. That source is the most sensitive area of the Canadian polity: the relations between French- and English-speaking Canadians and, more particularly, the relations between the federal government at Ottawa and the government of the province of Quebec. Never have federal-provincial relations been so unsettled, so complicated, and even so strained as they have been in the past two years. There is an obvious irony (though it is probably also a fortunate coincidence) in the fact that the governments of both Canada and Quebec are Liberal and that the Prime Minister of Canada, Lester Pearson, and the Premier of Quebec, Jean Lesage, were colleagues in the St. Laurent government before the Conservative victory in 1957.

The tensions between Quebec and Ottawa must be seen in a wide perspective. In the first place there is a kind of rhythm in the Canadian federal system in which periods of centralization are followed by provincial revolt and decentralization. The years between 1939 and 1957 were characterized by vigorous federal leadership and the dominance of Ottawa. Quebec never accepted this centralization fully, though its attitude was ambiguous: it consistently elected a firmly provincial autonomist Union Nationale government in Quebec, but just as regularly re-elected the supporters of the centralizing Liberals at Ottawa. By the mid fifties provinces other than Quebec were

growing restive under federal tutelage and the number of
provincial Conservative régimes increased. John Diefenbaker successfully took advantage of this provincial unrest in his campaign to dislodge the twenty-two-year-old
Liberal régime in 1957.

The Diefenbaker victory had a peculiar effect on
French Canada. The slim 1957 success was won despite
Quebec, which clung to its traditional Liberal allegiance.
But that election frightened French Canadians, for it
proved that a federal election could be won virtually
without the support of Quebec. It was a long time since
the minority position of the French Canadian had been so
graphically illustrated. In 1958, however, the situation
was rectified when the Diefenbaker landslide included a
Conservative majority in Quebec for the first time since
1887. But the apparent strength of the Conservative Party
in Quebec was misleading. In the first place the Quebec
wing of the federal party included almost no one of experience who could both state Quebec's case in the federal
cabinet and fulfil his ministerial duties effectively. The one
man who might have played that role, Léon Balcer, had
opposed John Diefenbaker's candidacy for the party
leadership and was therefore somewhat under a cloud.
The result was that the Diefenbaker government was never
en rapport with the aspirations of French Canada.

The lack of French-Canadian leadership in the Conservative government reflected something that proved an
even more serious weakness: Conservative electoral
strength in Quebec was built on the shakiest of foundations. In Quebec there had been no provincial Conservative party since it merged with a group of dissident Liberals in 1935 to form the Union Nationale led by the one-
time Conservative, Maurice Duplessis. In 1957, and
especially in 1958, the federal Conservative Party suc-

ceeded where it previously had failed in obtaining the support of the Union Nationale machine. The alliance was an unnatural one based only on a common hostility to the Liberal Party. The result was that the Union Nationale, an ardently French-Canadian nationalist party, helped send to Ottawa French-speaking Conservatives whose intense autonomism was bound to make them unhappy in a party dominated by Diefenbaker's 'one Canada' philosophy. It is not surprising that one French-Canadian Conservative backbencher was, in 1961, openly describing Confederation as a 'fool's paradise' for Quebec.

The Diefenbaker landslide in Quebec in 1958 bore within itself the seeds of its own destruction. The Union Nationale, which had held power in Quebec since 1944, had become a corrupt, autocratic, and intensely conservative régime, which stayed in office by skilfully playing on traditional French-Canadian fears of an Ottawa dominated by the English-speaking majority. Since the federal government was Liberal, Duplessis convinced Quebec voters that provincial autonomy could only be defended by keeping the provincial Liberals out of power. But once Diefenbaker had removed the Liberal menace from Ottawa the old game could no longer be successfully played. This gave the provincial Liberals a new lease on life, which they grasped impatiently. For several years, under the guidance of the impressively intellectual but cold George Lapalme, the party had been building up an organization and defining a progressive program. At the same time it was losing elections. In 1958 the crushing defeat of the federal Liberals made an extremely dynamic young politician available to the provincial party. He was Jean Lesage, a capable, attractive former cabinet minister, well known as a persistent spokesman for Quebec's interests in Ottawa. Doubtless when Jean Lesage took over the leadership of the provincial Liberal party, one of his main concerns was to rebuild the fortunes of his party at Ottawa. But a series of unpredictable events thrust him into power in Quebec in less than two years.

In 1959 the Union Nationale experienced almost unbelievable bad fortune. First its founder and leader, a man who had been a true 'chef' in the French-Canadian tradition – Maurice Duplessis – died. His successor was a man more in tune with the times than the ageing Duplessis had been. But Paul Sauvé, the new leader, had very little time in which to implement the progressive social ideas he subscribed to; before his first year of office was ended he suffered a fatal heart attack. This left the party in a state of internal strife, totally unprepared for the election of June 1960. That election brought Lesage to office in Quebec and marked the beginning of the end for the Quebec federal Conservatives, who could no longer rely on the formerly powerful Union Nationale machine for support.

Since Quebec's voice was so ineffectively expressed in the Conservative cabinet at Ottawa, many French Canadians, after 1960, turned their eyes to Quebec City for leadership. They were not disappointed. While Diefenbaker's government seemed bewildered in the face of the country's numerous problems, Lesage's Liberal *équipe* at Quebec was in the process of unwrapping a program of modernization designed to bring public policies into line with the economic and social developments of the previous twenty-five years. Before 1960 bright young French Canadians looked to Ottawa or to such federal institutions as the Canadian Broadcasting Corporation and the National Film Board as havens where they could express their ideas without fear of the penalties which the Duplessis administration used freely against its critics. Now these people found their province, and especially the provincial government, anxious to make full use of their talents. A new atmosphere of freedom seemed to prevail in Quebec and at last it was possible to question every traditional institution, including Confederation itself. Some of the noise in today's Quebec is the sound of exploding myths, some the noise of a society working furiously to modernize itself, and some an old noise rejuvenated: nationalism.

The death of Duplessis removed a cap that had kept the seething discontents of French Canada sealed up for more than a decade. It is doubtful if even Duplessis could have kept the cap on much longer, for the social and economic forces at work were much too potent. Quebec, like so much of North America since 1940, has experienced a period of accelerated industrial and urban growth. While this was not the sudden process that is sometimes suggested — the stereotyped *Maria Chapdelaine* view of Quebec's Arcadian culture has been outdated since the twenties — there can be no doubt that the war and post-war economic boom transformed Quebec into a society very much like Ontario or the eastern United States in its social organization. This economic development was carried out very largely through the investment of non-French-Canadian capital. The result was that class lines and 'national' lines tended to coincide. Moreover, Quebec remained remarkably backward in adopting the kind of social welfare policies that make a modern industrial society acceptable to the great mass of the people who live in it without owning much of it.

The fact was that the Union Nationale government's public philosophy was a nineteenth-century capitalist's dream: foreign capital was invited to a province with enormous natural resources, stable government, low taxes, cheap and largely unorganized labour. Premier Duplessis

consistently fought federal welfare policies as infringements on provincial rights, but rarely did he offer any
alternative policies of his own. The bitterly fought strikes
in Quebec in the forties and fifties were reminiscent of
the 1890s in other parts of North America. In these labour
disputes the Duplessis government openly identified itself
with 'foreign' capital against French-Canadian labour.
The enormous under-representation of urban areas in the
provincial legislature meant that the Union Nationale had
little to fear from the votes of angry trade unionists. Despite his reactionary policies Duplessis never failed to win
re-election through a combination of electoral corruption,
personal charisma, and an ear finely tuned to the frustra-
tions of French Canada's minority complex. He skilfully
used nationalism as a shield to protect his conservative
policies in the sham battles he fought against Ottawa,
while at the same time allowing the alienation of the province's economy. It is no wonder that in progressive circles,
both inside and outside Quebec, French-Canadian nationalism became highly suspect. An intellectual (who today
is a separatist of the socialist variety) wrote in 1958 that
'those who like me have experienced the bankruptcy of
what is called our "national doctrine" must seek a new
direction. They do not believe that the Nationalist orientation can ever produce a living culture, a living politics,
living men.'

In these years of Duplessis's ascendancy a new French-
Canadian middle class was spawned. This class was composed of people who in growing numbers were turning
away from the traditional professions of French Canada:
law, medicine, journalism, and the Church. Instead,
though only slowly because of the continued domination of
clerically-directed classical education in Quebec, the most
ambitious young people turned to business, engineering,

and the social sciences. These people, as well as many members of the traditional professions, began to look at society in a new fashion. Many of them discovered that to advance in their professions they had to adopt much of the culture of the dominant, English-speaking minority: they had to hang up their language with their coats at the office. The new nationalism of Quebec is partly a reflection of the tension created in the minds of young people who want both to succeed in their professions and also to maintain their culture.

It was these same people, the urban middle class, as well as the urban working class, who became increasingly critical of the out-dated social philosophy of the provincial government. They wanted the kind of positive state that would help them solve their problems by providing better educational opportunities, higher welfare benefits, better housing facilities, and equitable labour laws. If Quebec was to be modernized and if French Canadians were going to exercise any control over that society there was only one institution which could be used: the State. In the provincial government French Canadians unquestionably had an institution that belonged to them if they chose to use it. In the past the Church had been the major institution of *la survivance*; today it is the State. That is the real, indeed only, revolution that has taken place in Quebec. It is also at the root of the friction between the federal and provincial governments.

In the past French Canadians looked upon the State with a deep suspicion. For one thing the State had been for nearly a century after the Conquest an instrument of English domination. Then, too, the French Canadian, faithful to his church, believed that an active State could threaten the prerogatives of the Church. The Church rather than the State played the predominant role in the educational, medical, and social welfare fields. But the practical limitations of the Church grew increasingly obvious as the traditional parish organization disintegrated under the impact of industrialization and urbanization. By the end of the fifties the demand for State action was becoming irresistible. Today it is no longer resisted. René Lévesque described the new role of the State in his usual colourful way when he said: 'It must be more than a participant in the economic development and emancipation of Quebec; it must be a creative agent. Otherwise we can do no more than we have been doing so far, i.e., wait meekly for the capital and the initiative of others. The others, of course, will come for their own sake, not for ours. It is we alone, through our State, who can become masters in our own house.'

Traditionally, French Canadians believed that if they exercised control over their language, their laws, and their religion, their survival as a distinctive community would be guaranteed. Each of these categories was placed in the hands of the provincial government at Confederation. But in recent years it became patently obvious that survival was endangered by economic and social changes. Economically and socially Quebec was becoming indistinguishable from English-speaking North America. Was cultural assimilation an inevitable consequence? If the answer was to be no, French Canadians realized that new instruments of survival were necessary.

The Liberal Party, elected in 1960, reflected this new attitude and indicated a willingness to translate it into policy. It reflected more than it created the attitude, and there can be no doubt that many, though not all, of Premier Lesage's ministers have seen the State move into areas that they would not have anticipated five years ago. Like any other democratic government, the Lesage cabinet is a coalition of different shades of opinion stretching over a fairly broad spectrum from moderate left to moderate right. There can, however, be no doubt that the left has asserted its ascendancy within the cabinet. And it is no accident that as it has shifted leftward it has also grown more nationalist. In both respects it reflects the changing temper of the province.

The first two years of the Lesage government saw a general cleaning up of corruption, the enactment of several social welfare measures and labour laws, and increased concern with education. But in 1962 a new departure was taken with the decision to nationalize eleven private hydro-electric companies, thus completing a step begun in 1944 with the creation of Quebec Hydro. It was the radical intellectual, René Lévesque, Minister of Natural Resources, who was the author of this policy. Its main intention was to give the government control of an industry that was fundamental to the economic development of the province. But while the decision was economic, it was also nationalist. In the 1962 election, called as a referendum on power nationalization, the Liberals campaigned on the slogan 'Maîtres chez nous'. The success of this appeal clearly showed that although nationalism under Duplessis may have been somewhat discredited among intellectuals it was far from dead among the populace. Indeed, under Lesage, and particularly under Lévesque, nationalism has been divested of its reactionary image and given a progressive façade and content. But the fact is that the Liberals appeal to the same sentiment of nationalism that Duplessis exploited so successfully. The difference is in the means proposed to guarantee *la survivance*; no public man in Quebec ever questions the end.

The positive nationalism of the Lesage government is

expensive. To extend welfare benefits, nationalize hydro, improve and increase the civil service, enter directly into economic expansion, extend and reform education — all require the expenditure of huge sums of money. In its search for revenue Quebec found that nearly every source was already being tapped by Ottawa. Since the Second World War Ottawa had grown accustomed to initiating the country's major welfare and developmental policies. While the Quebec government had often objected, Ottawa usually proceeded in one fashion or another. Moreover, ever since the wartime and 'cold war' emergencies, Ottawa has kept a tight-fisted control on all the major sources of revenue. The Lesage government, autonomist from the start and nationalist to an increasing degree, quickly made plain its unwillingness to accept passively either Ottawa's exclusive initiative in developmental policies or its primacy in the fields of direct taxation. While the Diefenbaker government moved slightly in the direction of decentralization, this was meagre in comparison with the galloping pace of the Quebec government's reforms and expenditures.

While the friction between the Lesage and the Diefenbaker governments at first had the appearance of a traditional quarrel between Liberals and Conservatives, Premier Lesage completely dispelled that notion in his budget speech delivered on April 5, 1963. He made it clear that his government was so committed to autonomy and to costly reform measures that it would expect whichever party was in power in Ottawa to meet Quebec's fiscal demands in twelve months. This statement, widely described as an 'ultimatum', was delivered three days before the voting in the federal general election. Since it was widely expected that the Liberals would be called upon to form a government in Ottawa after the election, the 'ultimatum' came as a shock to many federal politicians. In fact, it was a shrewd declaration of independence. If the Liberals were elected, Lesage wanted it to be perfectly clear, especially to the voters of Quebec, that his government would not be a mere handmaiden of federal policies. That declaration of independence has since been made formal by an almost complete separation of the federal and provincial party organizations in Quebec. Though this move shocked many English Canadians, its real purpose was nothing more than to destroy the bogey of federal domination that the Union Nationale had used so effectively against the provincial Liberals in the past.

Premier Lesage's insistence on the independence of his party was an accurate reflection of the new mood of the province. This new mood manifested itself in a profound suspicion of the federal government. Ottawa's reputation reached an all-time low during the last year of the Diefenbaker régime, and nowhere was its reputation worse than in Quebec. But while the federal government could be restored to a place of honour in English Canada, the malaise was deeper in Quebec. After the death of Duplessis a new generation of Quebeckers began to make their voices heard. Though the majority of these people found their views well represented by the Lesage government, and especially by the voluble René Lévesque, there were others who were discovering new forms of radicalism that could be fitted into the old nationalist moulds. Everywhere in Quebec after 1960 there was a questioning of traditional values. The traditional role of the State was rejected, the place of the Church in society and the layman in the Church questioned, the purposes of education endlessly debated, and, naturally, French Canada's position in Confederation was examined. There seemed so many necessary tasks to be undertaken in Quebec itself that many French Canadians lost interest in the rest of Canada. Then, too, there were those who concluded that the source of Quebec's problems was Confederation itself.

There have always been people in Quebec who have believed that French Canada's ultimate salvation could only be achieved if the full status of independent nationhood was acquired. But these groups, in the past, have never been strong. Today they represent, according to the only serious analysis that has been made, something like thirteen per cent of the population of Quebec. Of these separatists the vast majority are well educated, below thirty, with a prosperous family background. They are, in fact, typical middle-class students and young professional people. Like the ideologically-minded everywhere, these young radicals reject the compromises and scorn the pragmatism of their elders in the Lesage government. Where Lesage cautiously develops the interventionist state, the radicals call for full-scale socialism and *planification*; where Lesage carefully increases State control over the previously Church-controlled educational system, the radicals advocate complete secularization or *laïcisme*; where Lesage defends his province's autonomy, the impatient youth demand national independence, or *séparatisme*. The separatist movement, which has never yet entered politics actively, is divided within itself, expressing views stretching all the way from a tiny fringe of terrorists, through Marxist anti-clericals, to clerical corporatists on the far right. All, despite effusive democratic professions, verge on a totalitarianism enforced on them by their commitment to nationalist absolutes. It sometimes appears that this young generation of anti-clericals has rejected the absolutes of the Roman Catholic faith only to accept the absolutes of a nationalist faith. Nearly all of their writings show an intense interest in the newly independent nations of Asia and Africa, a profound ignorance of economics, and a pride in the achievements of contemporary France.

Despite the widespread publicity the separatists have gained, partly as a result of tight organization and youthful enthusiasm and partly as a result of scattered acts of violence, the movement does not command broadly based support in Quebec. Its strength could grow rapidly, however, if the Lesage government lost its reform impulse, or if English Canadians refused to respond to the moderate demands for change being made by the provincial Liberal government. At the moment, both of these dangers are present, but not threateningly so. If the movement was to grow it would have to spread into the working-class population of the province. So far the working people have remained largely immune to separatism, suspecting that they would have to pay the undoubted price that separatism would entail. The leaders of the two major trade union organizations have made their opposition to separatism unmistakably clear. Jean Marchand, leader of an exclusively Quebec union, stated just over a year ago that in his view Quebec's problems had very little to do with the constitution. It goes without saying that the business community and those responsible for the province's economic growth are opposed to separatism, which they fear may discourage investment in Quebec.

Separatism, with its several faces, is only one political manifestation of Quebec's contemporary social turmoil. A no less striking phenomenon, and one based on much wider electoral support, is *créditisme*, the Quebec version of the economic heresies of Major Douglas. Where separatism is the panacea offered by the ambitious middle-class intellectual as a solution for all Quebec's problems, *créditisme* has found its main support among the lower middle class and the urban and rural lower classes. But, like separatism, *créditisme* is a symptom of the revolt against the old order.

Until 1962 no federal party other than the Liberals and Conservatives had ever made any appreciable impact on the French-Canadian voter. Yet in the 1962 federal election twenty-six Quebec constituencies returned Social Credit members. The leader of the party was a fiery, demagogic automobile dealer, Réal Caouette, who admits a one-time admiration for Adolf Hitler and Benito Mussolini. While Caouette, unlike most English-Canadian supporters of the Social Credit Party, is a true Douglasite monetary reformer, his main electoral appeal was the slogan 'Vous n'avez rien à perdre.' Much of his party's vote came from people who were disillusioned with the Conservatives without having been won back by the Liberals. What the Social Credit vote seemed to exemplify was a rootless, aimless, *poujadiste* discontent with the status quo among people whom Premier Lesage's sophisticated reformers had failed to reach.

Like every other group in present-day Quebec, Réal Caouette's party soon became afflicted with *nationalisme*. By 1963 Caouette had broken with the English-Canadian leader of his party, forming a separate Quebec group. While it is not a separatist party, its concern for monetary reform has been largely replaced by rather confused demands for constitutional reform. It is unlikely that the *créditiste* party will survive much beyond another election. In the meantime, however, it stands as an unsettling reminder of the ease with which discontented people can be attracted to a properly presented slogan.

Both separatism and *créditisme* represent in extreme form the intensity of the nationalist impulse in Quebec and the widespread dissatisfaction with the social, economic, and political status quo. Although the source of much of this discontent is in Quebec society itself and can therefore only be removed by the provincial government, there is an inevitable tendency to blame Confederation itself. While the vast proportion of Quebeckers reject separatism at present, there are very few articulate French Canadians who are satisfied with the existing position of the French Canadian in Confederation. A host of suggestions to rectify the situation have been made. Few are very specific, and of those, most seem impractical or unacceptable from the English-Canadian viewpoint.

Currently a view put forward by several vocal groups in Quebec is that an entirely new constitution should be devised to meet the needs of the 'two nations' in Canada. Under this new constitution each nation would have its own sovereign state, but the two would be associated in a loose confederal arrangement, each represented equally, and each having the right of veto. This theory of 'associate states', though it seems to have won the vague approval of two members of the Quebec provincial cabinet, has very little prospect of acceptance. In the first place, Premier Lesage himself is realistic enough to know, and to have said so publicly, that the time is not ripe for full-scale constitutional revision. English Canada remains largely unconvinced of the need for radical constitutional change. Moreover, there is a committee of the Quebec legislature currently examining a wide range of proposals for constitutional change, and the government will certainly not commit itself before that committee has done its work. Finally, on the basis of the meagre details of the 'associate state' theory that have so far been presented, it is fairly clear that it would create economic chaos and endless political instability. It is, in fact, only a thinly disguised form of separatism.

For the immediate future the present constitutional

structure, modified substantially in its workings, offers considerable hope. In the current parlance the new approach is called 'co-operative federalism'. In general this means a commitment by the federal government to the decentralization of responsibilities and revenues and close, almost continuous, consultation between the federal and provincial authorities on nearly every aspect of policy. This even includes federal-provincial meetings on such unquestionably federal responsibilities as international trade. What it means above all is careful, detailed negotiations rather than rhetorical appeals to 'national unity' and 'provincial rights'. Some French Canadians suspect this highly empirical approach as another Anglo-Saxon ruse. But the well-trained civil service that has been built up in Quebec, as well as the highly responsible French-Canadian politicians at both Ottawa and Quebec, recognize that it is the only realistic approach, given the mood of English as well as French Canada. Like most Canadian public policies, 'co-operative federalism' is really another word for compromise. Maurice Lamontagne, one of Prime Minister Pearson's closest French-Canadian advisers and chief author of the new approach to federal-provincial relations, said recently that 'Confederation . . . remodelled to establish a balance of forces which form our country and to satisfy to a greater extent Quebec's aspirations is, I feel, the only real hope of the French Canadians. It is the only way to a mutually acceptable compromise. Co-operative federalism is half way between federalism *de tutelle*, which existed until 1963 but which is no longer acceptable to French Canadians, and confederative federalism which is no longer satisfactory for present-day problems and which the English Canadians would not accept.'

A second aspect of the new approach to relations between French and English Canadians is a clear commitment on the part of the federal government to improving the status of French Canadians in federal institutions. More French Canadians are being appointed to better civil service posts, and more important, French is gradually becoming a more 'normal' language in the public service. The Royal Commission on Bilingualism and Biculturalism is investigating the whole range of problems relating to French-English relations. The French-speaking co-chairman of this commission is André Laurendeau, one of the most intelligent and respected men in Quebec. As the editor of the nationalist Montreal daily *Le Devoir*, Laurendeau never failed to defend Quebec's autonomy or the rights of French Canadians. But he was also an effective opponent of separatism, the more so, no doubt, since he himself had been a separatist in his youth in the thirties.

The commission has the task of examining the place of French and English Canadians, as well as the role of the numerous ethnic groups or New Canadians, in Canadian society. Its most difficult and at the same time most important task will be to consider the treatment of the French-Canadian minorities outside of Quebec. Here it will be concerned with one of the oldest and most bitter grievances of French Canadians. While the English-speaking minority in Quebec has a completely separate educational system and constitutionally guaranteed bilingualism, the seventeen per cent of French Canadians who live outside Quebec have no such privileges. In some provinces bilingual schools exist in a limited way – in Ontario, New Brunswick, and Saskatchewan – but they are precarious and sometimes impose extra tax burdens on French and Catholic parents. While French Canadians have long asked for more equitable treatment, the response from English Canada, until recently, has been negative. Today many French-Canadian nationalists, particularly those of the separatist variety, advocate the abandonment of the minorities to inevitable assimilation. For many separatists, the opposite side of this coin would be a unilingual Quebec. Most French Canadians, however, remain reluctant to accept this attitude, believing that the minorities are a part of the French-Canadian nation and that it would be immoral to abandon them. As for the minorities, there is no stronger anti-separatist group in Canada than the leaders of the French-speaking Acadians in New Brunswick.

The problem of the minorities will receive a great deal of attention from the Royal Commission. The difficulty will arise, however, when the time comes to implement the commission's recommendations. Many of these recommendations will doubtless relate to educational matters and that is a wholly provincial concern. The fact is that English Canadians have not yet come to accept the view that French Canadians are different from other minority groups and therefore have a right to special treatment. Yet the solution to the present crisis in Canada depends in large part on the practical acceptance of the fact that Quebec is not a province like the others, and that the French-Canadian minorities are not minorities like the others.

The resolution of the current difficulties depends on both the federal and Quebec governments. Perhaps more on the latter than the former, for the source of the problem is economic, social, and educational more than constitutional. But there is always the danger that the more impatient, more ideological groups will force the Quebec government to turn its eyes from practical reforms to constitutional debate. There is also the danger that the anti-French-Canadian voices in English Canada will grow so strong as to convince the moderate people of Quebec that there is no real hope of two nations living peacefully within the bosom of a single state. Both these dangers are increased by the instability of the minority government at Ottawa.

Still, the readjustments that have already been made are reasons for optimism about the future. The Canada that emerges from the present heated debate will be a different country, and probably a better one to live in. And there can be no doubt that the change will be largely the result of the transformation that has taken place in Quebec. René Lévesque summed up that change in an interview just over a year ago when he described his province as 'a nation awake, in full swing, fed up with being seen as a museum, as "the quaint old province of Quebec"; a nation bent on advancing, rising, no longer just content to endure'.

If Quebec nationalism becomes too assertive and self-centred it will undoubtedly stimulate an equally self-centred and assertive response from English Canadians, in which case the country will face a crisis unlike anything it has ever witnessed before. Contrary to the general belief, Canada's problem is one of too much nationalism, not too little. Indeed, the central paradox of the country is that its unity is strongest when its various nationalisms remain muted. 'The Canadian state cannot be devoted to absolute nationalism, the focus of a homogeneous national will,' a distinguished Canadian historian wrote two decades ago. 'The two nationalities and four sections prevent it.' That is the hard truth that Canadians are trying to relearn today.

TWO

Quebec, Ontario, and the Nation

Once, in the not very distant past, Quebec and Ontario had images of one another that reflected profound differences of outlook. The Ontarians' caricature of the neighbouring French-speaking province was that of a society symbolized by the soutane and the chalice: a 'priest-ridden province'. Quebeckers had an equally striking mental picture of Ontario: a society of *orangistes*. There were also some more secular, though no more complimentary, aspects to this picture. For Quebeckers, Ontario often appeared as a community of money-loving materialists – a characteristic well known to go hand in hand with the dour anti-Catholic Calvinism of the province. For Ontarians, Quebeckers just as often appeared as inefficient, unimaginative *habitants* who never succeeded in business because – it was well known – Catholics invested their money in churches rather than in factories. Again, the French Canadian frequently viewed his Ontario compatriot as 'imperialist', more loyal than John Bull himself. The counter-image which flashed through the Ontarian's mind was that of the disloyal French Canadian who was anxious either to destroy the British connection completely or so to weaken it as to render it ineffective. Finally, and this brings us closer to the present, there has long been a suspicion in Ontario that French Canadians want either to force everyone to speak French or, by *la revanche du berceau*, to swamp Ontario. The French Canadian, in turn, suspects that Ontarians are open or secret believers in the total assimilation of the Quebecker.

Like all popular mythology, these images contained elements of truth. There was also much, of course, that was based on sheer prejudice and ignorance. But what is important is not the accuracy of the images but the fact that people accepted them as a part of the picture of the world in which they lived. At bottom, these mythologies were part of the nationalisms of the two peoples, an expression of each one's belief in its superiority over the other. It was to these basic, if often unconscious, stereotypes that politicians, preachers, priests, and journalists often appealed when Canadian public questions were discussed. It is this popular psychology that lies behind the more prosaic events that make up the history of the relations, political, cultural, and economic, between Quebec and Ontario within the structure of the Canadian nation since Confederation.

Confederation was much more a response to the needs of Canada East and Canada West than to those of any other part of British North America. To put it simply, these two colonies, which had been united in a legislative union since 1841, wanted to get free of one another by the 1860s. This was especially true of Ontario, many of whose leaders were firmly convinced that their section laboured under an enormous and growing injustice in a union where each province was represented equally in the legislature despite a growing disparity in the populations of the two communities. Canada East, with its unique culture, could never agree to George Brown's demand for 'rep by pop' unless an alternative to legislative union was devised. Therefore, federation, either of the two Canadas or of all British North

America, seemed the answer. This arrangement would provide for local control over local affairs by the establishment
of provincial governments, and representation by population in a new federal legislature.

It is sometimes claimed that federalism was our fate in
Canada because of the needs of Quebec for autonomy in
matters relating to *la survivance*. That is true, but only
partly so. To suggest that Ontario preferred legislative
union is to mistake the views of John A. Macdonald and
his supporters for those of all Ontario. And that is a mistake no Grit could ever forgive. The Reform party, led by
George Brown and the Toronto *Globe*, had constantly insisted on the need for local autonomy for Ontario; at the
Great Reform Convention of 1859 the party came within
an ace of declaring for complete dissolution of the union.
At its convention called to prepare for action in the new
Confederation in June 1867, the Ontario Reform Party
again plighted its faith in 'local control over local affairs'.
To ignore the strength of this sentiment in Ontario is to
make it impossible to understand why, four years after
Confederation, the Reform Party, the party of provincial
rights, gained power in Ontario and remained there for
thirty-four years. It took Quebec, the province always
dubbed 'autonomist', until 1886, fifteen years after Ontario, to elect the party that placed 'provincial rights' at the
top of its electoral program.

The father of 'provincial rights' in Canada, if the members of the Judicial Committee of the Privy Council are
declared ineligible, is not Jean Lesage, Maurice Duplessis,
Alexandre Taschereau, Sir Lomer Gouin, or even Honoré
Mercier. He is Oliver Mowat, Premier of Ontario during
the most critical twenty-five years of Canadian history,
1871-96 – years during which the new system, in Macdonald's phrase, 'stiffened in the mould'. For fifteen years

Mowat fought almost alone, aided occasionally by Nova Scotia which periodically threatened secession, against what he viewed as federal paternalism. He fought Macdonald over the status of the lieutenant-governor, over the federal power of disallowance, over the question of whether the federal or the provincial government should have the power to enforce prohibition (no one seems to have suggested that no government should have that power!), and over the question of the rights of Liberal lumber barons to use streams improved by Conservative lumber barons. While he cannot be said to have won his battle for provincial autonomy single-handedly, since the Judicial Committee of the Privy Council gave his position an enormous assist, it can be said that he received precious little help from Quebec before 1887.

When the hanging of Louis Riel, combined with other local factors, brought Honoré Mercier's *Parti national* to office in Quebec in 1886, Mowat at last had an ally. But the first combined campaign, in which Nova Scotia, New Brunswick, and Manitoba joined, was largely a failure. That was the Interprovincial Conference of 1887, called by Mercier and presided over, owl-eyed, by Oliver Mowat. At that conference Quebec had one major interest: increased federal subsidies. Ontario, little interested in higher subsidies that would likely cost her more than she received in the long run, demanded a series of constitutional reforms designed to limit the power of Ottawa. The two types of demand, financial and constitutional, were combined in a series of resolutions which Macdonald and the federal government ostentatiously ignored.

While the 1887 conference failed to achieve its immediate goals, it was nevertheless a political success. It had brought together the provincial barons who now made their Liberal party ready for a renewed assault on the Conserva-

tive King John A. In 1896, with Macdonald five years
dead, the Liberal assault on his old party was a complete
success. So great was Laurier's indebtedness to the provincial barons that he included three of the five premiers who
had caucused in 1887 in his cabinet: Mowat of Ontario,
Fielding of Nova Scotia, and Blair of New Brunswick.
Norquay of Manitoba was the one Tory who had dared to
attend the Interprovincial Conference and he had passed
from power by 1896. Mercier, the fifth premier, had been
dismissed from office by a lieutenant-governor who suspected him of corruption.

The provincial-rights axis established by Mercier and
Mowat has never been completely destroyed. With the birth
of provincial rights came also the birth of a constitutional
doctrine that has bedevilled Canadian history since Confederation. That theory is the compact theory, the view that
Confederation was founded upon an agreement among the
provinces and that it cannot be changed without the consent
of those provinces. Once again that theory, often attributed
to Quebec, probably found its earliest expression in Ontario, particularly in statements by Oliver Mowat and in
the editorial columns of the Toronto *Globe*. The most complete statement of that doctrine came from Howard Ferguson in his famous open letter to Prime Minister Bennett in
1930. At that date Premier Taschereau of Quebec was
quicker to express his support for the Ontario premier than
his predecessors had been in giving their support to Mowat.
Since Mowat and Mercier, then, there has been a traditional
alliance between Quebec and Ontario, an alliance that
shows no respect for party lines, for the defence of provincial rights. Whitney and Gouin associated closely together,
as did Ferguson and Taschereau, to say nothing of that pair
of lovelies, Hepburn and Duplessis. Indeed, though much
criticism of the report of the Rowell-Sirois Commission has

emanated from Quebec since 1940, its recommendations
were torpedoed in 1941 not by a Quebec premier (who at
that date was Adélard Godbout) but by Mitchell F. Hepburn. In his inimitable style, Hepburn characterized the
report as 'the product of the minds of a few college professors and a Winnipeg newspaperman who has had his knife
into Ontario ever since he was able to write editorials'.
Premier Duplessis in his most truculent mood never did
better.

Quebec and Ontario, then, have traditionally co-operated
in the fight for provincial rights and against centralization.
But have the motives of the two provinces been the same?
The answer is partly in the affirmative. Both provinces –
Ontario especially in the first fifty or so years of Confederation, Quebec throughout the century – have wished
to defend their particular identities and interests against
a homogenizing 'Canadianism'. Neither apparently felt
strong enough to make over Canada in its own image, so
each has attempted to maintain its particularism at home.
It might be argued that the apparent decline in provincial-
rights sentiment in Ontario in very recent years indicates
that Ontario now believes that it can dominate Ottawa and
the rest of Canada. But that argument depends on the
answer to this question: has Ontario really given up the
cause of provincial rights, or is the present posture of the
province merely a consequence of the general atmosphere
of decentralization, the heavy Ontario representation in a
minority government, and the 'coolness' of Mr. Robarts's
approach to politics?

More interesting and perhaps even more significant than
the common Quebec-Ontario stake in the cause of provincial autonomy are the differences. Again Quebec's insistence upon provincial rights has been largely based on a
desire to preserve the French-Canadian way of life, how-

ever that is defined. But from the time of Mowat to the present, Ontario has been conscious that as a rich province, it will be called upon to finance a large part of the programs of the central government whether these are federal subsidies and equalization payments or federally sponsored social welfare schemes.

It is almost an axiom of Canadian federalism that the poor provinces are centralists, the rich decentralists. Ontario is and always has been the wealthiest – though much of its wealth has been drawn from business transacted in other parts of Canada. Until recent years Quebec has not shared Ontario's view on fiscal matters, since it benefited, or at least did not lose, in the general sharing around of federal largess. As Quebec more fully exploits its economic resources, and as it moves forward in its attempt to develop a balanced economy equal to Ontario's, the two provinces' attitudes toward federal economic policies may grow increasingly alike. If that development takes place, it will represent a real danger to the less fortunate sections of the country. It was that concern that lay behind the recent remark of Nova Scotia's Premier Stanfield before a Montreal audience: since his province could not depend upon the assistance of the other provinces in the field of economic development, it therefore favoured a strong central government.

Historically, then, in the Canadian competition of nation versus province, Quebec and Ontario for various reasons have agreed that the federal government should not be allowed to swallow up the provinces. Both provinces have, of course, been interested in the nation as well as in themselves, and both have had strong views about the fashion in which that nation should develop. And on this question there has been serious conflict between the two provinces.

One of Ontario's chief motives in supporting the Confederation scheme was a desire to expand both physically and economically. By 1867 Ontario farmers were hungry for new lands; they looked enviously at the western lands which remained under the control of the Hudson's Bay Company. Moreover, Toronto businessmen were anxious to expand their economic empire. George Brown and the Toronto *Globe* voiced both these aspirations. After Confederation had been achieved and steps taken to acquire the west, the *Globe* delineated Ontario's ambitions when it remarked: 'We hope to see a new Upper Canada in the Northwest Territory – in its well-regulated society and government, in its education, morality and religion.'

That was a worthy enough aim, provided that it was forgotten that probably a majority of the people in the Northwest in 1869, excluding the Indians, did not subscribe to English-speaking Protestant Ontario's views on 'education, morality, and religion'. Most of the inhabitants were half-breeds and Métis, and at least in Manitoba a majority were Roman Catholic. One needs only to mention the hanging of Louis Riel, the attack on the French language in the Northwest Territories in 1890, the interminable controversy over the abolition of separate schools in Manitoba, and the storm that broke over the Autonomy Bills in 1905, to indicate that Ontario largely succeeded in creating a 'new Upper Canada in the Northwest'. Indeed, in the new territories, Ontarians, with large-scale assistance from immigrants from the United States, Great Britain, and Europe, achieved what many Ontarians would have liked for their own province: a state system of unilingual schools. But the constitution guaranteed separate schools in Ontario – though the French language was another matter, and served as the source of the fierce controversy that swirled around Regulation XVII during the Great War.

Quebec's concept of Canada was very different. There is

no doubt that Cartier hoped that Manitoba would develop along the lines of Quebec. That is why the Manitoba Act of 1870 recognized the separate-school system in the province and made French an official language in its public affairs. Similarly the early history of the Northwest Territories was characterized by a recognition of the bicultural character of the community. But Quebec was not an expansionist province, at least not physically. Its economic expansion was directed by that complex of English-Canadian financiers connected with the Canadian Pacific Railway and the Bank of Montreal. Despite repeated appeals from politicians, and especially from Church leaders like Archbishop Taché of St. Boniface, very few French Canadians migrated to Western Canada. They preferred, apparently, to follow Curé Labelle into the northern regions of Quebec or, in even greater numbers, to try their hands at fortune-making in the mill towns of New England. Nor could the French Canadian, in contrast with his English-speaking compatriot in Ontario, rely on outside sources to swell his numbers. Frenchmen for the most part refused, understandably, to leave 'la douce France' for an unknown future on the Canadian prairies. Undoubtedly the Canadian government did not work as assiduously as it might have to attract French-speaking immigrants. It is equally true that many leaders of the Church in Quebec were just as glad that not too many of the inhabitants of the 'godless republic' found their way to Canada. But whatever the causes, the fact is that when the great waves of hungry immigrants began to flood the fertile western plains after 1890, there were precious few French sounds in the babel of tongues that was heard.

Everywhere it was Ontario-type democracy that triumphed, a democracy that emphasized individual rights and opposed group rights. In the Anglo-Saxon 'Kulturkampf' which was designed to 'Canadianize' immigrants, French-speaking settlers were rarely differentiated from Germans, Poles, Ukrainians, and so on. By the end of the First World War, George Brown's dream had been accomplished and Cartier's hopes crushed.

Of course, the responsibility for this development cannot be laid entirely at Ontario's door. It was the inhabitants of the western provinces who themselves chose to pattern their provinces on Ontario and the United States. Nevertheless they were frequently encouraged by influential journalists like John Willison of the Toronto *News*, and by magazines like the Toronto *Saturday Night*, which declared during the debate on the Autonomy Bills: 'In the last analysis the question to be answered is: Shall the Roman Church be established as a Government institution, supported by Government funds, with the Hierarchy of that Church forming the real Government by which the affairs of the country are conducted?' Remarks of that sort naturally produced heated responses in Quebec. Armand Lavergne, a young nationalist, condemned the Autonomy Bills for failing to give Saskatchewan and Alberta constitutions modelled on Quebec. He declared: 'In constituting the French Canadian, who has lived in the country since its discovery, the equal in rights and privileges to the Doukhobor or the Galician who has just disembarked, we have opened between the Eastern and Western sections of Canada a gulf that nothing will be able to close.'

No incident did more to colour the attitudes of Quebec and Ontario towards one another than the struggle over Regulation XVII, formulated by the Ontario Department of Education in 1912. While controversy still surrounds this regulation, its effect, if not its intention, was to limit the rights of French-speaking Ontarians to receive their education in the French language to the lowest forms of primary school. As early as the 1880s Ontario had been the scene of a 'No Popery' campaign, which coincided with an outburst of cultural conflict in the rest of the country. The agitation against separate schools and bilingual schools gained impetus from an action taken by Honoré Mercier which satisfied many Ontarians that Quebec was a theocracy. In 1888 Mercier settled a long-standing problem concerning the estates confiscated from the Jesuit Order at the time of the Conquest. He determined to compensate the Jesuits, but in order to avoid entanglement in the process of making the division of the funds among various religious bodies, he provided for arbitration by Rome. Part of the response to this action was a demand for federal disallowance of the statute. That demand received the support of only thirteen federal M.P.s, all from Ontario. A second illustration of the response was the cry that French-language schools be outlawed. But despite the dire warnings of the Toronto *Telegram* that force might be necessary 'to teach Quebec that the purpose of Confederation was the upholding of a free, not a French, nation on one half of the continent', Premier Oliver Mowat stood firm in his defence of the rights of the Franco-Ontarians.

By the end of the first decade of the twentieth century, however, the situation had drastically changed. The most important aspect of this change was the large increase in the number of French-speaking people in Ontario, Quebeckers who had spilled over into the eastern and northern sections of the province. The *Orange Sentinel*, while not a typical Ontario newspaper, was nevertheless an important one in the years before the First World War. Its comment on the growing French population was unequivocal: 'It is part of the great ambition of the French that French be equal with English. Should that demand ever be conceded

. . . the battle waged for a century will have been lost, and the barrier that Ontario has for so long opposed to the oncoming tide of French settlement will have been swept away. All that would mean to the destiny of Canada cannot be readily imagined. It would almost inevitably mean French domination and papal supremacy.'

From 1912 to 1916, when the Judicial Committee of the Privy Council ruled that Regulation XVII was valid, the battle raged, often with ferocious intensity. The Legislature of Quebec interfered directly in the affairs of Ontario first by passing a resolution expressing the hope that the grievances of the Franco-Ontarians would be redressed, and a year later by authorizing Quebec school commissions to contribute directly to the Franco-Ontarian cause. Henri Bourassa and his friends condemned Ontarians as 'Prussians'. Armand Lavergne wounded the sensibilities of patriotic Ontarians with the following outburst delivered in the Quebec Legislature: 'If the Germans are persecutors,' he declared, 'there are worse than persecutors at our very gates. I'll go further. I'll say that every cent that is spent in Quebec to aid enlistment of men is money stolen from the minority in Ontario. . . . I ask myself if the German régime might not be favourably compared with the Boches of Ontario.'

The dispute was thus at its bitterest at one of the most crucial stages of the war, and it led directly into the even more divisive debate over conscription in 1917. The blunt opposition of most French Canadians to conscription confirmed Ontarians in the belief that Quebeckers were either disloyal or cowards or both. Once the war was over, however, normal relations were fairly quickly restored. By 1927 Regulation XVII, which had never been successfully enforced especially in Ottawa, was withdrawn. The controversy over conscription during the Second World War reawakened some old hatreds and suspicions, but the stark division of 1917 was not reproduced.

One final example of the conflict between the Quebec and Ontario concepts of Canada is provided by an exchange in the House of Commons in 1927. The two members involved were not completely typical of their compatriots. Yet both carried to a logical conclusion views that were held in moderate form by a great many of the inhabitants of their respective provinces. The Ontario member was Horatio Hocken, Conservative member for Toronto West Centre. Before the war Hocken had combined his occupancy of the editor's chair at the *Orange Sentinel* with the position of Mayor of Toronto. By 1927 he had lost some of his earlier Orange fire, but his basic convictions about the nature of Canada were unchanged. His counterpart was Henri Bourassa, once again a federal M.P., now nearing the end of his editorship of *Le Devoir*. Some of the fire had gone out of him too, but he still believed as strongly as ever in a vision of Canada almost exactly the opposite of Hocken's. The exchange took place during the debate on a private member's motion which proposed the granting of preferential treatment to bilingual candidates for the federal civil service.

In opposing the resolution, Hocken expressed a widespread English-Canadian viewpoint:

. . . it must be plain to anyone who understands English that this is not a bilingual country. . . . We contend that this proposal is an attack upon the English-speaking people of Canada, an attack upon the rights of every English-speaking young man and young woman, for it forces them either to learn French or to keep out of the civil service. . . . Ontario and the other provinces are not aggressive against their sister province of Quebec. It is that certain leaders in Quebec are aggressive against the other provinces, and will not observe the conditions of the act of confederation.

Bourassa replied, saying, as he had so often said in the

past, that the spirit of the constitution was one of Anglo-French equality. He continued:

The province of Quebec is not a French province, and the reason why the provincial spirit is still kept up in that province is precisely that attitude of mind, on the part of a certain number of English Canadians who consider Quebec as apart from Confederation just as, for example, some Indian reserves are kept apart for the preservation of the remnants of our aboriginal races. The province of Quebec is one of the nine Canadian provinces. The vast majority of its people speak French, but they grant to the English-speaking minority the right to speak English freely, and they accord them in the local administrations, municipal or provincial, those facilities which we ask in federal affairs, not merely as a matter of right — I would never put the question on that narrow basis — but as a matter of common sense, and true Canadian spirit, so as to spread out into every province of Canada the same spirit of Canadian citizenship which exists in Quebec, and should exist everywhere in the Dominion.

Time has been kind to the views of Henri Bourassa; it has been harsh to those of Horatio Hocken. But that should not be allowed to disguise the fact that both, in their times, gave expression to sincerely held views — views that may have represented minority schools of thought only because of their frankness. Today Hocken's position seems to be disappearing in Ontario. Is Bourassa suffering the same fate in Quebec?

One last aspect of the relations of Quebec and Ontario in the Canadian nation is the respective roles they have played within the federal political parties. Since Quebec is not a province like the others, it might be expected that in federal politics it would usually find itself in opposition to the other provinces. The fact is, of course, very different. Only in 1911, 1917, and 1957, in this century, have Quebec voters sent a substantial number of their members to the seats to the left of Mr. Speaker in the House of Commons. Ontario, on the other hand, has much more often swelled the ranks of the opposition, before 1896 with Liberals and since then most often with Conservatives.*

The explanation of this phenomenon is extremely complex. The mechanics of Canadian federalism seem to work best when the ruling party combines a majority in Quebec with majorities in the Maritimes and the West. That represents a rough description of the Liberal party of Laurier and King. The combination is based, in part, on the desire of the smaller and economically weaker provinces to check the strength and economic ambitions of the most powerful province. The system works worst when a government is formed out of a solid delegation from Ontario and large numbers of members from the other English-speaking provinces. That is a description of the Borden government of 1911 and even more accurately of the Union government of 1917. It might be argued that the system works nearly as badly when both Quebec and Ontario send majorities to the government benches. That is a description of Mr. Diefenbaker's government of 1958 and Mr. Pearson's 1963 government. Although the latter case was complicated by the government's minority position, it does not

*This generalization has some important exceptions. The Canadian voting pattern from 1867 to 1896 suggests a fairly even division of the parties in both Ontario and Quebec, with both provinces giving majorities to the government of the day. The pattern was broken in 1891 when Quebec turned slightly Liberal. Laurier, however, never once won a majority in Ontario though he came very close in 1896. It was chiefly Ontario that defeated him in 1911. In the inter-war years the pattern was roughly the same, with Quebec a Liberal preserve and Ontario favouring the Conservatives, though R. B. Bennett made some gains in Quebec in 1930 and then lost Ontario as well as the rest of the country in 1935. King managed to hold both Ontario and Quebec in 1940, but lost Ontario in 1945. Mr. St. Laurent held Ontario and Quebec in 1949 and 1953 but lost Ontario in 1957, and Mr. Pearson lost Quebec in 1958. In 1962 Mr. Diefenbaker lost Quebec and Ontario. (See H. A. Scarrow, *Canada Votes*, New Orleans, 1961.)

seem too fanciful to suggest that part of its ambiguity on many issues was the result of the Quebec-Ontario tension within it. It might even be worth suggesting the hypothesis that the strength of Ontario in the last three governments is one of the causes for Quebec's suspicions of Ottawa. What neither Mr. Diefenbaker nor Mr. Pearson seems to have known is that Mackenzie King, before every election, silently petitioned his deity for a Conservative victory in Toronto, for that guaranteed a Liberal victory elsewhere. And King usually found that Toronto would elect at least one Conservative member who caused his own party more trouble than he did the Liberals—a Horatio Hocken, a Tommy Church, or a Dr. Herbert Bruce. That Mr. Pearson has not understood this rule is best illustrated by the presence of Ralph Cowan in the ranks of the Liberals!

There have, of course, been good reasons for the division of Quebec and Ontario in federal politics. There is, for example, the obvious fact of metropolitan competition between the country's two largest cities, Toronto and Montreal. In recent times these differences, which were once exemplified in the competition between the Montreal-based Canadian Pacific Railway and Bank of Montreal and the Toronto-dominated Bank of Commerce and Canadian Northern Railway, have been seen in the controversy between Mr. Walter Gordon and Mr. Eric Kierans. A newspaperman's report of an interview with Mr. Kierans in September 1965 began with the following paragraph: 'Quebec is out to regain its place in the sun – the Canadian sun – and Montreal is out to regain its financial leadership from Toronto, according to Quebec Revenue Minister Eric W. Kierans, former president of the Montreal and Canadian Stock Exchanges.'

Secondly, the division is cultural, and this has been reflected in the differing views about the shape that Canadian society should assume. Since the federal government was one of the main instruments for the building of this society, the competing ideas were repeatedly expressed at Ottawa, though in the last analysis the decision was often determined by the type of available immigrants. It is at the level of nation-building that one of the main paradoxes of Canadian politics is manifest. While the Western provinces and the Maritimes were usually willing to combine with Quebec to hold Ontario's imperial ambitions in check, they were rarely willing to accept French-Canadian views on the bicultural nature of Canadian society. When it came to the discussion of the place of the French language in Canada, a Western radical like J. S. Woodsworth, or a Western Liberal like Sir Clifford Sifton, agreed not with Bourassa but with Hocken.

Perhaps if the economic goals of Ontario and Quebec were to develop in a complementary direction, the two central provinces could also agree on a pattern for national development that would be more *bourassiste* than hockenesque. But until that Utopia is achieved, it is perhaps worth recalling that a distinguished western Canadian editor, J. W. Dafoe, once argued that the only thing that saved the country from disruption was 'the failure to get the two central provinces together in a single party'. He added an observation that remains as pertinent now as it was forty years ago: 'Policies that do not command a reasonable measure of support in each of the provinces', Dafoe wrote, 'are obviously not national and can only be enforced at the country's peril.'

THREE

Quebec and Confederation: Past and Present

The political problem of the French-speaking minority in Canada is as easily defined as it is difficult to solve: how can a self-conscious minority preserve its distinctiveness in a community governed by the principles of majority rule and representation by population? Clearly in such a society if a public question arises which divides the community along cultural lines French-speaking Canadians inevitably find themselves subjected to what is sometimes called 'the tyranny of the democratic majority'. Such issues have arisen in Canadian life in the past — most seriously in 1885 over the hanging of Louis Riel, during the First World War crises over French-language schools in Ontario and conscription for overseas service, and again over the conscription issue during the Second World War. These crises, which seriously ruptured relations between French and English Canadians, suggest that in Canada something more than simple majority support is necessary if public business is to be transacted smoothly and efficiently. A rough consensus of opinion in both French and English Canada is a primary requirement. The achievement of that consensus has been the objective of most of our political leaders. And the very machinery of government in Canada was, in part, designed to help make that consensus possible.

When the Fathers of Confederation sat down at Charlottetown and later at Quebec to formulate the principles of union for British North America, one of the first problems they had to grapple with was that of the place of a minority in a majoritarian state. There were, of course, several types of minorities, including, in Sir John Macdonald's view, the rich.* But the most important minority was French Canada. It was not only the spokesmen of French Canada who insisted that the new state be a federal one, but they were certainly the strongest proponents of federal as opposed to legislative union. George Etienne Cartier, the leader of the French-Canadian delegation, told the Quebec Conference: 'We thought that a federation scheme was the best because these provinces are peopled by different nations and by peoples of different religions.'

What federal union provided was that French Canadians, while participating fully in all the common affairs of the new nation, also had one province where they would be in a majority. And the provinces were given control over those matters which, in 1867, seemed most important for the preservation of French Canada's distinctiveness – education, civil law, and matters respecting religious life. Thus, in addition to being a union of the four provinces, Confederation was also a division between Canada East, or Quebec, and Canada West, or Ontario, which had previously been united in a single legislative union. Hector Langevin predicted, too optimistically as events were to

---

*Macdonald is reported as saying: 'A large qualification should be necessary for membership in the Upper House, in order to represent the principle of property. The rights of the minority must be protected, and the rich are always fewer in number than the poor.'

prove, that 'in Parliament there will be no questions of race, nationality, religion, or locality, as this Legislature will only be charged with the settlement of the great general questions which will interest alike the whole Confederacy and not one locality only'.

At the same time, French became one of the two official languages of the federal parliament and its records or journals, and of the federal courts. Quebec, alone among the provinces, was made bilingual in its legislature and in its courts. In this sense, as in one or two more minor matters, Quebec was not to be a province like the others. Something that is not always realized is that it was not until 1867 that French became constitutionally one of the two official languages of Canada. French had been used in public business before Confederation, but it was not until the passage of the British North America Act that it obtained legal recognition as an official language.

Despite the federal structure of the new nation and the guarantees given to the French language, by no means all French Canadians were enthusiastic supporters of the new constitution. Many of them feared that their minority position would be more vulnerable than ever in an arrangement that united the Canadas with the maritime colonies and looked forward to the addition of the Prairie West and the Pacific Coast territories in the near future. Moreover, there was a strongly expressed opinion that the new federal scheme placed so much power in the hands of the central government that a legislative union, in all but name, was in fact being established. The future of French Canada would thus rest at the mercy of the central power where English Canadians would always be in a majority. A.-A. Dorion, a leading opponent of the proposed Confederation, expressed these fears when he stated:

I know that majorities are naturally aggressive and how the possession of power engenders despotism, and I can understand how a majority, animated this moment by the best feelings, might in six or nine months be willing to abuse its power and trample on the rights of the minority, while acting in good faith, and on what is considered to be its rights.

Dorion was worried, moreover, by the talk that he heard from the supporters of Confederation about a 'new nationality'. Did this mean a uniform nationality? Did it mean the assimilation of French Canada into an English-speaking melting-pot? It fell to Cartier to deal with these charges. He affirmed that a new nation was being projected but it would be a political nation which allowed for, indeed encouraged, cultural diversity. 'The idea of unity of races was utopian,' he said; 'it was impossible.' As to French Canada's minority position, Cartier had two answers. First he said that the real question before Canadians was whether they would 'obtain British North American Confederation or be absorbed in an American Confederation'. Of these alternatives, Canadian federation was the obvious choice. Then, turning to the question of French Canada's role in the central government, the tough, cocksure Cartier noted that there would always be French Canadians in the cabinet and they would be backed by a phalanx of sixty-five French-Canadian votes in the House of Commons.

While there was no popular vote on the Confederation scheme, the parliamentary division of the members from Canada East in 1865 was very close – twenty-seven in favour of the plan, twenty-two opposed to it. Perhaps François Evanturel, a French-Canadian Conservative, expressed the views of many of his people when he remarked:

I am in favour of the principle of Confederation, and one of those who maintain that by means of that principle the rights and liberties of each of the contracting parties may be preserved; but on the other hand, I am of opinion . . . that it may be so applied as to endanger and even destroy, or nearly so, the rights and privileges of a state which is a party to this Confederation. Everything, therefore, depends upon the conditions of the contract.

In the first ninety years after 1867 both the supporters and the critics of Confederation were provided with some evidence to support their predictions. There can be no doubt that French Canadians benefited from the new arrangement. They shared in the economic progress that the new country experienced. They took an active part in the formulation of those policies which were designed to acquire full legal nationhood for Canada. Within the province of Quebec, French Canadians were their own masters in political and cultural matters. Economically they did not have full control over their society, but the complicated explanation of that situation had little, if anything, to do with Confederation.

But French Canadians also suffered set-backs and disappointments in the new federal structure. And as set-backs were experienced attempts were made to devise new methods of solving the old problem of minority rights in a majoritarian state. The first serious crisis arose in 1885 when the Macdonald cabinet, including three French Canadians, decided to allow Louis Riel's death sentence to be carried out. Riel, the enigmatic, unbalanced Métis leader of two rebellions in Western Canada, became a symbol of the renewed strife between French and English Canadians within the new federation. To many English Canadians, Riel was the murderer of a young Ontario Orangeman during the Red River Rebellion in 1870. To many French Canadians, the Métis leader was a valiant, if misguided, defender of a French and Catholic minority in Western Canada.

Though strongly opposed to the decision to allow Riel to hang, Macdonald's French-speaking colleagues did not resign from the cabinet, thus hoping to prevent the division

of the country into warring cultural factions. Nor were
the sixty-five Quebec members of parliament numerous
enough, or united enough, to punish the government with
defeat. What French Canadians were brought to realize,
probably for the first time in 1885, was that when an issue
divided Canadians along French-English lines, English-
speaking Canadians were the majority and could control
decisions at Ottawa. This realization caused French Canadians to look inward and to fall back on their provincial
government as the one bastion protecting them against the
English-speaking majority. In 1885 French Canada found
in Honoré Mercier a new leader and one who was, significantly, a provincial politician who had opposed Confederation. 'We feel', Mercier declared in 1885, 'that the murder
of Riel was a declaration of war on the influence of French
Canada in Confederation, a violation of right and justice.'
Taking advantage of the emotions aroused by the Riel
affair, Mercier called upon French Canadians to cease their
'fratricidal quarrels' and form a solid 'national', that is,
Quebec national, front.

It was Mercier who, as premier of Quebec, provided the
first important expression of a view of Confederation that
has become a standard French-Canadian interpretation.
This was the 'compact theory' of Confederation, a theory
which insists upon the 'autonomy' of the provinces. Shortly
before Mercier's election, a Quebec judge, the Hon. T. J. J.
Loranger, had worked out this theory in considerable detail. His essential argument was that 'the Confederation of
the British provinces was the result of a compact entered
into by the provinces and the Imperial Parliament which,
in enacting the British North America Act, simply ratified
it.' Moreover, the judge argued, the provinces in setting up
the federal government had only delegated certain powers
to it. Therefore the provinces were not only autonomous

but, as the creators of the federal government, were equal rather than subordinate to it. If the autonomy of the provinces was not recognized, he concluded, the road to a fully centralized legislative union was a short one.

One interesting point about Judge Loranger's exposition of the 'compact theory' was that he made no effort to prove that the compact was an agreement between French and English Canadians. For him the compact was among the provinces regardless of cultural differences. Perhaps the reason for this attitude was that Judge Loranger was really taking his cue from the Premier of Ontario, Oliver Mowat, who throughout the 1880s was engaged in legal combat with the federal government over a series of questions relating to the powers of the provinces. The Liberal premier of Ontario, like the Conservative prime minister of Canada, was one of the Fathers of Confederation. But the two founders differed seriously over the role of the provinces in the new federation. It is worth emphasizing that the doctrine of provincial autonomy found its first effective exponent in an English-speaking premier of Ontario. The French-Canadian Judge Loranger was merely urging Quebec politicians to join Mowat in the struggle against Ottawa.

Mercier, on becoming premier in 1886, quickly accepted the advice; for Ottawa, having bloodied its hands in the Riel affair, could now be easily stigmatized in Quebec. Together with Oliver Mowat, Mercier arranged a conference of provincial premiers in 1887 for the dual purpose of proposing limits to the powers of the federal government, particularly the power to veto provincial legislation, and also to press the federal government for larger financial subsidies to the provinces. Not all of the provinces attended the Interprovincial Conference, a fact which made it easier for Sir John Macdonald to ignore the meeting's resolutions. But the standard of provincial rights had been firmly planted in 1887. Moreover, an unofficial alliance between the country's two largest provinces had been established, an *ad hoc* alliance which in the twentieth century was occasionally renewed by Premiers Taschereau and Ferguson, and Duplessis and Hepburn.

But despite alliances of this kind, Quebec has always had a unique interest in its defence of provincial rights. That interest was Quebec's distinctive French and Roman Catholic culture. Nothing stimulated Quebec's fears of English Canada more than the attacks, beginning in the 1880s, that were made on that culture where it existed in pockets outside of the province of Quebec. Beginning with the abolition of state-supported separate schools in Manitoba in 1890 and stretching through to the tragic years of the Ontario school controversy during the First World War, the rights of the French-speaking minorities were gradually whittled away. Although these beleaguered minorities, supported by Quebec leaders, fought back vigorously, their numbers were small and their opposition numerous. Section 93 of the British North America Act, which gave the federal government power to initiate remedial action when the legitimate school rights of a minority were interfered with by a province, remained a dead letter. The reason was quite simple: the use of the power was politically dangerous for English-speaking politicians, and French-speaking representation at Ottawa was too small and too divided to force remedial action. Ironically, it was Wilfrid Laurier and the Liberals who prevented a Conservative government in 1896 from taking action to restore minority rights in Manitoba.*

*Sir Wilfrid Laurier to the end of his life insisted that Cartier had been mistaken in agreeing to give the federal government this power to interfere in provincial affairs.

Whatever the explanation for the ineffectiveness of the federal remedial power, there can be no doubt that the efforts to limit French rights outside Quebec caused French Canadians to look more and more to their own province as the only part of Canada where they were fully at home. As Edmond de Nevers noted in 1896 in his book *L'Avenir du peuple canadien-français*, 'The Northwest is closed to us, thanks to the unjust retrograde law passed by the Legislature of Manitoba prohibiting French schools. . . .'

Nevertheless, it was during these years of crisis over the rights to the French-language and Catholic schools outside Quebec that the theory of the cultural compact of Confederation began to receive an explicit formulation. As early as 1890 when the attacks on these rights in Manitoba and the Northwest Territories were being mounted, Sir John Macdonald replied with his view that under the Canadian constitution all British subjects enjoyed 'equal rights of every kind, of language, of religion, of property and of person'. Macdonald, of course, was not speaking of a compact. But it was this very statement to which French Canadians like Henri Bourassa appealed in support of the theory of bicultural compact. 'The Canadian nation', Bourassa declared in 1917, 'will attain its ultimate destiny, indeed it will exist, only on the condition of being biethnic and bilingual, and by remaining faithful to the concept of the Fathers of Confederation: the free and voluntary association of two peoples, enjoying equal rights in all matters.' For Bourassa and his followers, Confederation was a federation of two cultures, as well as of provinces, in which French- and English-speaking Canadians had a moral claim to equality of linguistic, religious, and civil rights from coast to coast.

Bourassa and those who spoke of a 'cultural compact' described an ideal rather than a reality and their compact was one which carried moral rather than legal sanctions. The implications of this moral compact are made clear by André Laurendeau, who has written that 'if force of number alone rules the relations *between an ethnic majority and an ethnic minority* then a common life becomes impossible and only separatism remains. The minority must leave the house which has become uninhabitable.'

Thus, while French Canadians have insisted upon provincial autonomy, a position often supported by some English-speaking provinces, they have also developed the theory of the moral compact guaranteeing minority rights. But there have also always been those French Canadians who have rejected Confederation as a fool's paradise. Usually these have been isolated intellectuals such as Jules-Paul Tardivel in the latter decades of the nineteenth century and some members of *L'Action française* group in the nineteen-twenties, or idealistic young nationalists like Jeune-Canada in the thirties. The separatist argument has always been based on the assumption that French Canada is a nation which should acquire all the trappings of complete nationhood including an independent state. In his apocalyptic separatist novel of 1895, *Pour la patrie*, Tardivel wrote,

God planted in the heart of every French-Canadian patriot a flower of hope. It is the aspiration to establish, on the banks of the St. Lawrence, a New France whose mission will be to continue in this American land the work of Christian civilization that old France carried out with such glory during the long centuries.

Tardivel's theme was that Confederation was part of a plan for the ultimate assimilation of French Canadians and the next step would be legislative union. The other alternative, the one that succeeded in the novel, was of course the establishment of a separate French-Canadian, Catholic state. Tardivel thus set the pattern for later separatist groups, most of whom have argued that Confederation will ultimately lead to legislative union and assimilation. In the nineteen-thirties separatists frequently warned against the argument that centralization was necessary to deal with the social crisis of the depression. Others contended that the defence and extension of provincial autonomy was a necessary first step toward an independent Quebec.

In the years before 1960 the voices of separatism had very little direct influence on Quebec politics. Nevertheless, the Quebec Legislative Assembly once debated a separatist resolution. In January 1918, a few months after the English-Canadian majority had insisted on conscription for overseas service despite the opposition of most French Canadians, J. N. Francoeur presented the following resolution to the provincial legislature: 'That this House is of opinion that the Province of Quebec would be disposed to accept the breaking of the Confederation Pact of 1867 if, in the other provinces, it is believed that she is an obstacle to the union, progress and development of Canada.' It is probably too strong to describe this motion as a separatist resolution and the debate that followed was characterized more by sorrow than anger. Not a single voice was heard in support of separation, and the motion was never brought to a vote. Sir Lomer Gouin, the premier of the province, could hardly have spoken more firmly of his faith in Confederation. He began by noting that 'federal government appears to me the only possible one in Canada because of our different races and creeds and also because of the variety and multiplicity of local needs in our immense territory'. He said that if he had been one of the Fathers of Confederation he would have attempted to win a better guarantee for French-speaking minorities, but he added: 'Even if it had not been accorded to me I would have voted in favour of the Resolutions in 1864.'

Despite this reaffirmation of Quebec's faith in Confederation, in the years after the Great War the French-speaking province was more jealous than ever of its autonomy. These were the years when Canadians began to expect government to play a larger role in social and economic affairs. And by government many English Canadians meant Ottawa. But French Canadians, still bitter about the conscription issue of 1917, retained a deep suspicion of any attempt by the federal government to increase its responsibilities. For example, Quebec remained out of the Federal Old Age Pension scheme, enacted in 1927, for more than eight years. Then, in 1936, the Quebec voters elected Maurice Duplessis, a premier who was to build his reputation as a staunch defender of provincial autonomy. Duplessis's party was characteristically called the Union Nationale and the national unity to which the title referred was that of Quebec, not of Canada. In 1938 Premier Duplessis refused to co-operate with the Royal Commission on Dominion-Provincial Relations established to examine the powers and responsibilities of all levels of government in Canada. Quebec's view was the traditional one: 'Confederation is a pact voluntarily agreed upon and which can be modified only by the consent of all parties.' Drawing out the implications of the 'compact theory', Duplessis's government, following in the tradition of Mercier, insisted that no alterations could be made in the Canadian federal system without the consent of all provinces. A few years later the Quebec premier explained why Quebec's autonomy was necessary, saying: 'The Legislature of Quebec is a fortress that we must defend without failing. It is that which permits us to construct the schools which suit us, to speak our language, to practise our religion and to make laws applicable to our population.' Here Duplessis was expressing the view of many French-Canadian nationalists that Ottawa was the government of English Canada while Quebec City was the government of French Canada. Underlying this view was the doctrine of two nations: Canadians and Canadiens.

Perhaps the event that most encouraged French Canadians to think of the government at Ottawa as a power dominated by English-speaking Canadians was the conscription plebiscite of 1942. Many French Canadians believed that the pledge made by the King government, and very specifically by Ernest Lapointe, in September 1939, that there would be no conscription for overseas service, was a promise made to French Canadians. In 1942, however, the King government asked not French Canadians but all Canadians to release it from the pledge. One participant in the events of 1942 has since written: 'French-Canadian nationalists were opposed in principle even to the plebiscite. They denied that the government should ask the majority to remove a pledge made to the minority. They denied in advance the validity of the Canadian response.'* The outcome of the plebiscite was what F.-A. Angers called 'un vote de race' with more than eighty per cent of French Canadians casting a negative ballot. King's handling of the conscription crises was almost unbelievably adept, so adept that French Canadians are convinced that the crisis took place in 1942 while English Canadians are equally convinced that the date was two years later. The fact is that unlike 1917 when all the poison was administered at once, King, in typical fashion, prescribed two half doses. The result was that the federal Liberal Party continued to thrive in Quebec despite the demise of Premier Godbout's fragile

---

*It is worth noting, however, that this argument based on the idea of 'compact' was not used by La Ligue pour la Défense du Canada in its 'Manifeste au peuple du Canada' in 1942, which went out of its way to emphasize the Canadian rather than the French-Canadian character of its appeal.

provincial Liberal administration. Nevertheless, the fact remained that when limited conscription for overseas service was adopted in late 1944 the English-Canadian majority imposed its will on the French-speaking minority. To many French Canadians the moral, as M. Laurendeau has written, seemed to be that 'at Quebec one does what one wants, at Ottawa one does what one can'.

In 1944 the Union Nationale was returned to power in Quebec. During the next dozen years the struggle between Quebec and Ottawa was intermittent but unceasing. These were years during which many English Canadians, at least, were becoming convinced that 'Canadianism' had at last triumphed over the country's chronic sectionalism, and only just in time, too, in the face of the growing threat of what many saw as subversive American cultural and economic influences. The report of the Massey Commission epitomized this spirit. But these same events caused profound uneasiness among French-Canadian nationalists who, in turn, feared that 'Canadians' might engulf 'canadienisme'. Premier Duplessis's battle against Ottawa thus won the support of the possessors of these disturbed nationalist consciences. Even so convinced an anti-separatist and vigorous critic of *duplessisme* as André Laurendeau was moved to write in 1955: 'The separatist policy has become a chimera and an absurdity. However, those who have a conscience very alive to the perils into which the policies of Ottawa over the past fifteen years have plunged us, and who are consumed with impatience, prefer absurdity and chimera to death.'

It was during these Duplessis years that the doctrine of 'two nations' received its full-blown exposition and, to some extent, obtained the official imprimatur. The doctrine received formal sanction in the voluminous *Report of the Royal Commission of Enquiry on Constitutional Problems* in 1956, which was, in effect, Quebec's answer to the report of the Rowell-Sirois Commission and Ottawa's post-war economic, social, and fiscal policies. The report of the Tremblay Commission included lengthy philosophical, sociological, and even theological discussions of the nature of the French-Canadian identity. But its fundamental postulate was that

... by reason of its history, as well as of the cultural character of its population, Quebec is not a province like the others, whatever may be said to the contrary. It speaks in the name of one of the two ethnic groups which founded Confederation, as one of the two partners who officially have the right to live and expand in this country. It is the only one able to represent one of the two partners, just as it alone may determine its reasons for refusing federal largess.

But the French-Canadian nation did not live exclusively in Quebec, and the report therefore advocated not only the limitation of federal powers but also the promotion of bilingualism and biculturalism throughout the country. And it put its finger on the central issue of Dominion-provincial relations when it remarked: 'There can be no federalism without the autonomy of the state's constituent parts, and no sovereignty of the various governments without fiscal and financial autonomy.' This was precisely the view that Premier Duplessis, with few philosophical trimmings, had been urging on the federal government for a decade.

While the autonomist theme was the predominant theme in Quebec during the fifties, it was not the only one. Indeed, the reactionary social policies and the growing corruption of the Union Nationale régime tended to discredit the provincial-rights cause in progressive circles. French-Canadian nationalism itself became suspect as a tool of reaction; the 'state of siege' mentality, it seemed, was encouraged as much to stifle reform in Quebec as to fight Ottawa.

In 1954 one reformer, Maurice Lamontagne, published *Le Fédéralisme canadien*, a careful study of the Canadian federal system which, in effect, advocated that Quebec accept fully the implications of the type of centralized federalism that the Rowell-Sirois Commission had recommended and that economic and social planning seemed to necessitate.

While Duplessis lived, neither the Tremblay Commission's theorists of 'positive autonomism' nor the propronents of what Lamontagne called 'une intégration lucide au nouveau fédéralisme canadien' gained control over provincial policy, though, of course, the former received a more sympathetic hearing than the latter. Undoubtedly far more important than the Union Nationale's constant, noisy war with Ottawa was the economic and social transformation that was taking place in Quebec and the gradual growth of a new nationalist impulse – one that was, at least in origin, more aggressive in its advocacy of social reform and in its defence of provincial autonomy than anything Duplessis had countenanced. Since 1960 the turmoil in Quebec has resulted in the revival of all the traditional attitudes toward Confederation, as well as some new ones, stretching all the way from 'co-operative federalism' and autonomism through to the idea of an associate state and separatism. The vague theory of an associate state includes among its proponents spokesmen for the traditionalist Société Saint-Jean-Baptiste, the populistic Créditistes, and the left-wing Parti Socialiste du Québec. The appeal of the doctrine of an associate state obviously lies in its ready solution to the problem of the relation of the minority to the majority without going as far as separatism. In brief, its proponents reject representation by population, whereby French Canadians are increasingly outnumbered, in favour of representation by 'nation'. It is, of course, a Canadian version of John C. Calhoun's 'concurrent majorities', though, strangely, one never sees any reference to the writings of the ante-bellum South's most distinguished theorists in the writings of French Canadians. At least to English Canadians, the idea of an associate state seems hopelessly utopian and perhaps even less acceptable than outright separation. In the first place, the idea would seem to promise only the deadlock which paralysed the union of the Canadas in the 1860s and led to Confederation. Secondly, French Canada's minority status is not as much the result of our present constitutional arrangements as it is of geography. No constitutional changes can alter the fact that French Canadians live in North America.

It is only the future, of course, that can supply fully satisfactory answers to the problems of the present. But the past suggests that it is in the realm of political action rather than in constitutional theorizing that solutions to our present discontents are likely to be found. It is highly significant that in his great struggle to defend the autonomy of his province against what he saw as the encroaching federal power, Premier Duplessis's chief antagonist was another French Canadian, Louis St. Laurent. And Prime Minister St. Laurent's position was characteristic. In the years since 1867 French Canadians have made their major adjustment to Confederation in the fashion that Cartier had recommended: effective leadership in the federal cabinet where an *ad hoc* system of concurrent majorities seemed at least partly feasible. A long line of vigorous French-Canadian politicians, beginning with Cartier himself and stretching through Laurier and Lapointe to St. Laurent, forcefully upheld the viewpoint of French Canada. It was in political action rather than in legal and moral compacts that these men placed their faith.* For them Confederation, while not

---

*Laurier and Lapointe (though not St. Laurent) subscribed to the 'compact theory', at least in a vague way, but to them the theory was obviously far less important as a device for defending French-Canadian rights than direct political action.

perhaps the ideal political arrangement, was nevertheless the best one available. All of them recognized that the relations between majorities and minorities in a democratic state can never be settled in an absolute manner. It was Sir Wilfrid Laurier who summed up this tradition best when he wrote just before his death:

There have been found among us limited spirits who have shouted very loudly, 'No compromise; all or nothing.' What an aberration! When a minority affirms that it will concede nothing, that it demands all or will accept nothing less than all, they are three times blind who do not see what the inevitable results will be: nothing. How can they not see that the majority itself will accept the doctrine and apply it without compunction to those who proclaim it! This truth was evident when Confederation was formed, it is equally so today. Salvation consists in administering Confederation in the same spirit as it was conceived, with firmness and always with moderation.

For Laurier, as for Cartier before him and Lapointe afterwards, Confederation was a compromise that provided for cultural coexistence within the bosom of a single political nation. Since the Canadian political community of 1867 had been established in a spirit of compromise it could only be operated effectively in the same spirit. That spirit meant that while the majority must respect the rights of the minority, the minority, for its part, can never forget that majorities also have rights. Only by working through the federal political parties in co-operation with English Canadians can French Canadians hope to have their viewpoint understood. Cartier had defined the underlying assumption of that co-operation when he declared in 1865: 'We were of different races, not for the purpose of warring against each other, but in order to compete and emulate for the general welfare.'

Since 1867 Canadian coexistence has not always been entirely peaceful, competition has sometimes been destructive. Yet, at least until recently, the overwhelming majority of French-speaking and English-speaking Canadians have remained convinced that Confederation, when operated in a spirit of 'firmness and moderation', has been a worthwhile experiment. It may not always be so, but until a more attractive alternative is offered it is perhaps well to remember a recent remark by a French-Canadian writer in summing up the Canadian experience. 'Most nations', he wrote, 'have been formed not by people who desired intensely to live together, but rather by people who could not live apart.'

FOUR

Quebec and Confederation:
A Look at Some Current Proposals

Over the past two or three years English Canadians have scarcely ever ceased asking French Canada what it wants. What Quebec wants, of course, is both simple and complex. Quebec wants equality for French-speaking Canadians. To say so, however, is a good deal more simple than to define the means of achieving that equality. Much is being done by the Quebec government itself to lay the basis for equality through reforms in the educational, economic, and social welfare fields. When the effect of these reforms, which are of necessity long-term in scope, is felt, some of the pressure for radical constitutional changes may disappear.

Currently, however, spokesmen for various groups in Quebec are advancing, with more or less clarity, several schemes for establishing political equality between French and English Canadians. This is not a new quest in Quebec and it is not one that is likely ever to be solved permanently. The question is of critical importance at present, however, because of the number of French Canadians who are obviously dissatisfied with the status of Quebec in Confederation.

The dilemma of French Canada in Confederation can

be simply stated: How can a self-conscious minority preserve its rights in a community governed by majoritarian
rules – that is, on the basis of representation by population? There have been in the past several responses to this
question. One answer was strong, united, French-Canadian
representation at Ottawa, and especially in the federal
cabinet. This is the Cartier–Laurier–Lapointe–St. Laurent
tradition. A second answer has been an emphasis on provincial rights in a federation which, in origin, was highly
centralized. This autonomist tradition, which began with
French-Canadian opponents of Confederation like A.-A.
Dorion, was first practised by the nationalist premier
Honoré Mercier in the 1880s and has been continued, to
a greater or lesser degree, by nearly every subsequent
premier of Quebec.

In the past the combination of these two techniques –
strong federal leadership and vigilant defence of provincial autonomy–worked fairly well. It did, however, involve
one contradiction that was never fully resolved. The
emphasis on provincial rights left French-speaking minorities in the other provinces at the mercy of English-speaking
majorities. It was the election of Wilfrid Laurier in 1896,
with the strong backing of Quebec, that in effect nullified
the federal power to protect minorities against provincial
infringements on their educational rights. For it was
Laurier who had attacked the Conservative attempt to pass
legislation forcing Manitoba to restore the minority education privileges that the Manitoba School Act of 1890 had
abolished. Constitutionally, the victory of Laurier and his
provincial-rights party in 1896 meant the triumph of provincial rights over minority rights. It is ironical, as the
nationalist Olivar Asselin pointed out, that 'this heresy was
first proposed by a French Canadian'.

As the vast majority of French Canadians live in Quebec,

it is not altogether surprising that provincial autonomy has always been their prime constitutional objective. Since 1960, however, there has been a growing belief in Quebec that the old methods of defending French-Canadian interests in Confederation are no longer effective. One of the reasons for this scepticism about the traditional combination of strong leadership in Ottawa and autonomy in Quebec is that it did, in fact, fail to work for a time. For whatever reasons, after 1957 the French-Canadian voice at Ottawa, especially but not only on the government side, was muted. At the same time an increasing number of Quebeckers were realizing that the autonomism of Premier Duplessis had been a good deal less rewarding than they had been led to believe. It was true, for example, that Premier Duplessis had protected the province's educational autonomy by refusing to accept federal grants to universities. But he had only done so at great cost to Quebec's educational institutions and taxpayers. Moreover, while Ottawa was being shut out at the front door, 'foreign' capitalists were being welcomed at the rear door as they rushed in to tighten their grip on the province's economy. To a generation increasingly concerned about economic and social problems, Duplessis's autonomist formula looked hollow indeed. Thus it appeared that Quebec had lost both its effective voice at Ottawa and control of the province's destiny. While there are several other factors underlying Quebec's dissatisfaction with her present status in the Canadian federal system, there can be no doubt that the breakdown of the traditional means of defence is a basic fact in understanding the host of constitutional panaceas that have recently been prescribed by French-Canadian intellectuals.

Believing that reform begins at home, the Quebec electorate ended the reign of the Union Nationale in June 1960. (Of course the defeat of the Liberals at Ottawa in 1957 was of enormous importance to the Lesage party, for it meant that the provincial Liberals could no longer be branded as the handmaidens of Ottawa's centralizing policies. Nor should the death of Duplessis or, nearly as important, the death of his successor Paul Sauvé be forgotten.) While it took some time for English Canadians to realize it, the new Liberal team's approach to provincial autonomy was quite different from M. Duplessis's 'everlasting no'. Premier Lesage attempted to approach federal-provincial relations from two directions. First, in Quebec, he intended to follow a policy of positive autonomism. This meant that instead of merely saying no to Ottawa, Quebec would offer alternatives. Thus Quebeckers would not be deprived of necessary services in the cause of provincial autonomy. The portable pension scheme is a recent example of this new approach of the Lesage government. On the whole the new attitude has been remarkably successful, so successful indeed that the attention of French Canadians has been turned away from Ottawa and what it represents, and towards *l'Etat du Québec* and what that could mean.

Premier Lesage's second approach to federal-provincial relations proved less successful. This was his revival of the inter-provincial conference which Honoré Mercier, along with Oliver Mowat of Ontario, had started in 1887 but which had long since fallen into disuse – a fate most federal politicians approved. Mr. Lesage apparently believed that the inter-provincial conference could assume a role in federal-provincial relations that would weaken the federal government without weakening Canada. Somehow, he hinted, the provinces together could initiate policies, perhaps in co-operation with the federal government, but which would be carried out by the provinces as national policies.

While the revival of the inter-provincial conference has been useful, and may prove more so in future, it has not lived up to Mr. Lesage's hopes. Partly this is because the Quebec premier never seemed entirely clear about the practical working of his scheme. And, of course, he was never entirely successful in convincing the nine other provincial leaders of the validity of his idea. This was unfortunate, for Mr. Lesage's conception of the inter-provincial conference was imaginative and might very well have restored the provinces to a more positive role in our federal system. More important, in the present context, the success of the inter-provincial idea might very well have made the search for other solutions to the problem of Quebec's relations with Ottawa less pressing. And most of the solutions now being proposed are far more threatening to the preservation of our federal system than the plan for provincial initiatives in national policy-making would have been.

It would be an oversimplification to suggest that it was failure of the inter-provincial conference scheme alone that produced the demand for more drastic constitutional changes. Even before 1960, and certainly ever since that date, voices in Quebec have been demanding a completely new constitutional deal for French Canadians. But the disappointingly meagre results of Mr. Lesage's first scheme have helped to swell the chorus of constitutional revisionists.

The major objective of the various current proposals is to answer the traditional question: How can a numerical minority exercise power equal or nearly equal to that of the majority? There are many answers being proposed in today's Quebec to this dilemma which is older than Confederation. One is to insist that Quebec is not a province like the others because it is the home of the French-Canadian nation. It must not, therefore, be treated on an equal footing with, for example, (the example always chosen by Quebeckers) Prince Edward Island. Somehow a constitutional means of making Quebec more than just one among ten must be found. But the question that arises, of course, is *how much* more than one among ten? And how, in our federal system, can one province be treated as more equal than others?

This is the conundrum that the architects of the rather ill-defined procedure of 'co-operative federalism' are attempting to solve. So far this concept implies gradual decentralization, the formula of consultation before decision (though consultation on what areas of federal power remains somewhat hazy), and the useful but obviously dangerous technique of the provincial right to opt out of joint federal-provincial programs without financial loss. In practice this last idea admits a special status for Quebec. But should other provinces, especially rich ones like British Columbia and Ontario, also take advantage of the formula, the whole program would collapse, leaving the have-not provinces in serious straits. It is not difficult to imagine how that would affect the attitude of Saskatchewan or Nova Scotia towards Quebec. Moreover, the position of the Quebec federal member of Parliament is, to say the least, anomalous when votes are taken on programs that Quebec has chosen not to join.

From Quebec's viewpoint 'co-operative federalism' may suffer from an even more serious drawback. It is based on constant negotiations, which, like all negotiations, will depend on the goodwill of the negotiators. Its operation lacks, and by its very nature perhaps cannot have, any formal constitutional guarantee. It has a political guarantee in that no government would be foolish enough, except in a mood of extreme crisis, to act directly contrary to the wishes of Quebec. But French Canadians are at present unwilling to accept a mere political guarantee. 'We need a Confederation', Pierre Laporte, the Quebec Minister of Municipal Affairs, said recently, 'which cannot be the prisoner of the good will or bad will of those who apply it.' French Canadians well remember the 1957 election in which, perhaps through no fault of their own, the Progressive Conservatives did the country the immense disservice of proving that a party can win power virtually without the support of Quebec. If this should happen again, some Quebeckers realistically ask, what would become of 'cooperative federalism'?

It is fears of this type, as well as many other considerations, that have pushed at least a minority of French Canadians into the acceptance of more radical schemes. The most clear-cut of these schemes is outright separatism. This is the solution advocated by people who refuse to believe that there can ever be a satisfactory working relationship between majorities and minorities. Most of these people seem to hope that at least on the economic level, close relations between French and English Canada would continue after separation. But, they say, we are two nations, English and French, so let us admit it in its fullest implications including political separation. To some extent, though not as much as their critics often think, the separatists overlook the problems that their solution would leave unsolved, to say nothing of those which it would create. Like ideologues of every type, separatists offer a simplistic explanation of political problems and pat, almost magical solutions that are the concoctions of closed minds that refuse to be confused by facts.

It is among people who accept the doctrine of two nations

but who realize the dangers of complete separation that yet
another doctrine of constitutional change has won support.
If Quebec is to achieve complete political equality, these
people hold, the system based on representation by population must be replaced by a system based on representation
by nation. Thus, the ratio of French to English would be
one-to-one. The constitutional application of this doctrine
has several variants, and in none has it been very specifically worked out. In the current jargon of Quebec constitutional discussion it is known as the concept of an 'associate
state'. The doctrine finds supporters across a wide spectrum
of Quebec's middle-class élite. René Lévesque and Pierre
Laporte, among the Liberals, have indicated general sympathy for the idea; Daniel Johnson and Jean-Jacques
Bertrand have been even more specific; Gilles Grégoire
has given the idea the *créditiste* imprimatur; and two
groups that would be expected to be poles apart – the
Montreal branch of the conservative Société Saint-Jean-
Baptiste and the radical Quebec Socialist Party – have
formally committed themselves to some form of 'associate
state' for their province. There are people who suspect that
when the Quebec Legislative Assembly's Committee on the
Constitution brings down its report in a year or so it will
recommend some version of this quasi-separatist idea. It
is important, therefore, for English Canadians to grasp at
least a general idea of the content of this phrase, which is
at present in some danger of becoming a cloudy, emotional
cliché.

The doctrine begins with the affirmation of the two-
nations thesis. No matter how loudly British Columbians
protest that Vancouver is not a subdivision of Toronto
or how clearly Newfoundlanders differentiate themselves
from mainlanders, the two-nations theorists insist that English Canada is a nation. 'I find', Jean-Marc Leger of *Le*

Devoir stated recently, 'rather puerile and sometimes not very honest the attitude which consists of attenuating differences between French and English Canada and exaggerating the regional distinctions among the English-speaking provinces with the intention of reducing the French-Canadian fact (or the "French-Canadian problem") and of presenting it simply as an aspect, the most significant, perhaps, but only an aspect, of "Canadian diversity".' (Evidently English Canadians who insist on their internal divisions are suspected of practising a most sophisticated version of the Machiavellian tactic of *divide et impera*!)

Having postulated the existence of two nations, the advocates of the 'associate state' idea argue that each nation must have full self-government (a doctrine they seem to confuse with self-determination). Therefore each state must be sovereign in a wide area including, it has been suggested, the acceptance of Quebec as an 'autonomous economic region' and an 'autonomous welfare state' pursuing its own policies in such fields as economic planning, banking, agriculture, natural resources, and social security. (In some of these areas, of course, Quebec is already relatively autonomous.) Moreover, Quebec would exercise certain powers in the field of foreign relations in matters relating to her own jurisdiction (this in addition, as we shall see, to an equal voice in the formation of foreign policy at Ottawa).

The sovereignty of the two national states would be limited by an agreement to establish a common central government, the unique feature of which would be equality of representation for each nation. The jurisdiction of this government would be narrowly limited to such matters as foreign and defence policy, international trade, postal services, transport, perhaps monetary policy, and the transfer of equalization payments from rich to poor sections of the Confederation. But more important than the specific fields of jurisdiction is the prescribed technique of policy-making and policy-implementation. Here, what amounts to a free, bi-national veto is introduced. In the view of the Société Saint-Jean-Baptiste of Montreal, 'No law would have force without being approved by a double majority, being a majority of representatives of each associate state.' Some other proposals, such as those of Professor Jacques-Yvan Morin of the University of Montreal's law faculty, are less radical in theory but probably no less so in practice. Professor Morin's plan would leave the basis of representation in the House of Commons unchanged, but it would transform the Senate into a Chamber of Nationalities exercising vague powers and representing each nation equally. More important is his suggestion that a number of boards, bi-nationally composed, would formulate policy and approve legislation before it was presented to Parliament. Thus, regardless of the representational basis of the House of Commons, the bi-national veto is clearly implied in this pre-legislative process.

A not entirely minor point is the question of what happens to the English and French diaspora – the minority groups – in a system that recognizes Quebec as one nation, English Canada as another. In Quebec the current fashion among separatists and quasi-separatists is to advocate writing off the French-speaking minorities everywhere except perhaps in New Brunswick. A corollary, sometimes unstated, is that Quebec should become unilingual (like English Canada) and eventually, no doubt, assimilate the minorities. The Montreal Société Saint-Jean-Baptiste apparently accepts this view. Professor Morin, however, provides for a section of his new constitution that would entrench minority rights. He even envisages a federal department of education (apparently under the control of the bi-national senate) which would assume responsibility for the education of French and English minority groups.

While no one as yet has fully worked out the details of the 'associate state' scheme, these general lines represent the essence. The most charitable interpretation that can be put on the idea is that it represents an admission, grudging as it may seem, that there is something beneficial in the political association of French and English Canadians. Less charitably it may be suggested that the advocates of the 'associate state' theory hope to avoid some of the obvious dangers of separatism by making a minimum contribution to the preservation of a Canada however disfigured. There is, of course, a third possibility, and that is that its advocates see the 'associate state' as the first step towards inevitable separation. In practical terms, this would halve the pain that a total break would doubtless cause. And the theory has a function of its own, inasmuch as the 'associate state' school provides a haven for those respectable intellectuals who do not wish to be branded as 'extremists'.

English Canadians, as Maurice Lamontagne recently warned, will almost certainly reject any proposal to revamp the constitution in the fashion proposed by the 'associate state' theorists. Indeed, many may find the idea so preposterous as to refuse even to consider it. The reaction of the Winnipeg editor who described the proposals put forward by the Montreal Société Saint-Jean-Baptiste as a 'prescription for national suicide' is doubtless typical. But there is a great danger in unconsidered rejection, for it would simply add weight to the claims of those French Canadians who insist that English Canada is rigid in its defence of the constitutional status quo and Quebec must therefore go its own way. Considering the present self-confident mood of Quebec, there is no reason to believe that the province's leaders have accepted the sober advice offered to them some years ago by Professor Michel Brunet. 'They must never demand of the majority', wrote the Montreal historian, 'that which the latter cannot give them.' It is surely wise therefore for English Canadians who are genuinely searching for a resolution to our present constitutional discontents to examine the 'associate state' proposals carefully.

From the viewpoint of English Canadians the fundamental assumption of the 'associate state' theory flies in the face of all that they have been taught about democracy. Their traditional belief is that while minority rights and opinions deserve protection and consideration, a democracy must be run on the principles of majority rule. To quote the realistic Professor Brunet again, 'A minority cannot lead a majority.' Moreover, rightly or wrongly, it would take a long time to convince English Canadians that their country can best be understood in the dualistic terms of the two-nations theorists. While not denying that injustices have been perpetrated against the French Canadians, particularly those outside of Quebec, English Canadians believe that both English and French Canadians have found it necessary to make compromises for the preservation of their common country. Most English Canadians would thus find the claim of the Montreal Société Saint-Jean-Baptiste that 'Each time so-called national unity has triumphed it is because French Canadians have bent before the English Canadians' a travesty on the Canadian experience and an irresponsible, indeed demagogic, generalization.

But even assuming that English Canadians willingly agreed to reject the past in favour of a new 'associate state' arrangement, it is extremely doubtful if any of our problems would be solved. There are reasons to suggest that the arrangement would emphasize most of our present prob-lems and create a host of new ones that would make our existing difficulties look minor indeed. On two general counts – one economic, the other political – the application of the 'associate state' doctrine could easily spell disaster for both French and English Canada.

It is surely not without significance that most of the makers of the new constitution of 'associate states' are jour-nalists, lawyers, and historians – one might almost say, the traditional élite of French Canada. All these are honour-able and even useful professions, but one wonders if they do not explain the ease with which the questions of the political economy of the modern state are passed over in the haste to condemn our present Confederation. Is there not a relationship between the economic life of Quebec and that of the rest of the country that is at once so close and so delicate as to make interference with the central mechanisms of economic guidance perilous in the extreme? There is, among the more progressive constitutional revi-sionists, an ability to speak with disarming ease about planning the Quebec economy. While an element of plan-ning at provincial and regional levels is doubtless possible and desirable in future, the interrelation of the various parts of the economy should never be ignored. Quebec and Ontario, the St. Lawrence system, have always been closely integrated. That was one of the reasons why Confederation was clearly preferable to separation when the Union of the Canadas began to fail in the 1860s. What was true then is no less true today.

It would be well for every advocate of the 'associate state' concept to start his discussion with a consideration of the recent study of the Quebec economy sponsored by the provincial Ministry of Industry and Commerce. In this study, *Croissance et structure économiques de la Province de Québec*, André Raynauld, assisted by two other professional economists, demonstrates with overwhelming evidence and superb professional skill that the Quebec and Ontario economies are tightly integrated in several major respects, and that no analysis of the Quebec economy can safely begin with the assumption of independence or isolation from the economy of North America. And those who cavalierly speak of economic planning should read with great care Professor Jacques St. Laurent's painstaking chapter on the possibilities of a Quebec steel industry. It is this type of study that once again illustrates that phrases like 'economic planning' and 'maîtres chez nous' are more easily pronounced than performed. And, as MM. Lesage and Lévesque demonstrated in their decision to place all of Quebec's hydro resources under public ownership, there is nothing in the British North America Act to prevent the fulfilment of the Quebec Socialist Party's objective of public ownership of the basic resources of the province.

If those who advocate fundamental reform of our constitution ignored the work of Professor Raynauld and his colleagues only at their own risk, there would be small cause for concern. But the risk is really to French Canada and Canada as a whole. It is more than a little irresponsible to suggest that constitutions can be made and unmade with little reference to the facts of economic life. If constitutional tinkering destroys the delicate balance of the Canadian economy, then Quebec's admirable effort to reform its public life and social institutions could well suffer irretrievably. And, of course, English Canadians would suffer just as seriously. While economic considerations alone should not govern French Canada's future, there is enough truth in the repeated claim of Quebec's 'new nationalists' – that survival without economic mastery is impossible – to give to constitutional discussions that ignore economics a sense of almost total unreality. Indeed there is even room for the suspicion that the 'associate statists' are more concerned about the French-Canadian nation than they are about French Canadians.

The question of economic decision-making laps over into the political field and raises an equally fundamental problem. In the proposed 'associate state' arrangement some economic decisions taken by the governments of the autonomous member states could seriously hamper federal policies. This, of course, is true even under our present arrangements. But in the new system, economic policy, like other policies, would be subject to the bi-national veto. A tariff desired by Quebec might be rejected by English Canada, ever conscious of the competitive position of her own manufacturers. A timber subsidy for British Columbia might be vetoed by Quebec representatives under pressure from French-Canadian lumber interests. And this points to the basic political weakness of the scheme: every issue would almost inevitably range French against English, Quebec against English Canada. The primary standard by which every public issue would be judged would be nationalist, English or French. Surely there is enough of that built into our society without making specific constitutional provision for it. The only real question about such a system would be, which side would reach the end of its patience first and call for the extermination of the two-headed monster?

In our present federal arrangement French Canadians have nearly always been able to find allies in some other part of Canada. That, of course, was the secret of success for the parties of Laurier and Mackenzie King. Their parties, in general terms, were coalitions composed of French Canadians plus enough support from the West and the Maritimes to prevent Ontario from dominating

Confederation. What Quebec's wisest politicians always realized in the past is that the salvation of French Canada lies in alliance with some part of English Canada. The Lafontaines of Quebec have nearly always been able to find a Baldwin in English Canada. In this way the majority has almost never coalesced against the minority on the federal level. But to institutionalize English Canada in a bloc, as the advocates of the 'associate state' plan would do, would likely end forever the possibility of this flexible type of political arrangement. Can anyone with even a fleeting acquaintance with the history of the cultural, political, and economic conflicts that shook the foundations of the United Canadas in the 1850s and 1860s really believe that an even more rigid system of bi-national vetoes and concurrent majorities could work? The Union of the Canadas with its equality of representation between Canada West and Canada East worked surprisingly well for a time. But there is a great deal of truth in the old saying that the real father of Confederation was deadlock. (And if examples of a system of free vetoes is wanted from further afield there is always the not very encouraging example of the Articles of Confederation, the loose arrangement that preceded the present Constitution of the United States.)

A new system, called 'associate states', would almost certainly lead to an impasse similar to that which paralysed the United Canadas by 1864. It seems highly unlikely, however, that a new deadlock would produce a new Confederation. Separation in anger, followed by the quite possible disappearance of French and English Canada, would be a far more likely outcome. In this event, many who at present look upon the 'associate state' concept as an alternative to separatism would wake up some morning to discover that they had bought a pig in a poke.

The details of the 'associate state' system, if they are ever worked out, might reduce the seriousness of some of these problems. It is equally possible that the details would only make the problem more obvious. In either event the importance of detailed discussion is obvious. At present the 'associate state' plan gives every appearance of being the product of fuzzy thinking. Intellectually and practically, it lacks the logic of either our present federal system or outright separation. In attempting to claim the best of both these worlds, in practice it would likely succeed in achieving neither.

Yet, even so, it should not be completely dismissed. Though the idea as currently proposed is obviously unworkable, it is representative of something very significant, and that is French-Canadian determination to alter Quebec's status in Canada. Proving that the 'associate state' formula is impractical will do nothing to undermine that determination. Many of the 'associate state' supporters are not objecting to Ottawa's existence, but they are decrying the feebleness of Quebec's influence on federal policies. This attitude at least hints that if Quebec's influence at Ottawa could be restored through less radical means, and if a recognition of Quebec's special status in Confederation could be achieved in a more practical fashion, then the 'associate state' theory would become irrelevant.

Moreover, there is a great danger in the present debate that we Canadians, French and English, may fall victim of the tyranny of words. What is needed in the present discussion is not slogans – and both 'co-operative federalism' and 'associate state' are in danger of falling into that category – but facts and detailed plans on which to base reasoned, informed negotiations. And we need also to remember, as the *mémoire* of the Montreal Société Saint-Jean-Baptiste pointed out in a moment of realism, that 'the true progress of a nation does not depend principally on constitutional texts'.

FIVE

Quebec: The Ideology of Survival

'Nobody in French Canada dares to think – at least nobody dares to think out loud,' a young French-Canadian teaching brother wrote in 1960. Soon, well over one hundred thousand copies of the book *Les Insolences du Frère Untel*, in which these lines appeared, had been sold in Quebec. The very response to Frère Untel's strictures was one evidence that a new Quebec, a Quebec eager for the full practice of freedom and democracy, and engaged in self-criticism, was suddenly emerging. 'We are afraid of authority; we live in a climate of magic where under penalty of death we must infringe no taboo, we must respect all the formulae, all the conformisms,' young Brother Jérôme continued. In his mind, freedom was available for the taking in Quebec, but the people were afraid of it. 'My own idea is that we are freer than we think, that it isn't liberty that is lacking, but the courage to use the liberty that we have. We whine about lost liberty, but don't use what we have. . . . Speaking as a Canadian, I say shall we take the plunge and be free?'

No one better epitomizes the new Quebec than Frère Untel, for despite the trouble with his clerical superiors that his unorthodox little book caused him, Brother

Jérôme's challenge was taken up by many of his compatriots. Today's Quebec is a society testing the freedom that Brother Jérôme claimed was present but unexercised. Today's Quebec is a society using that freedom to examine every aspect of traditional life, with the result that many standard assumptions have been rejected. The Church, the State, political parties, the educational system, the economy, and even Confederation have been challenged to justify themselves. Under the raucous noise of a Quebec undergoing a siege of self-criticism is a series of related economic and social changes which form the material basis of the new Quebec.

Ten years ago Professor Jean-Charles Falardeau of Laval University wrote: 'The daughter of Maria Chapdelaine who was an ammunition-factory worker at Valcartier during the war now lives with her own family of five children in the Rosemount ward of Montreal. Maria's married brothers are employees of the Aluminum Company at Arvida and Shipshaw after having been workers at the Jonquière pulp plant.' Nothing could more graphically sum up the change that has taken place in the province of Quebec than this imaginary epilogue to *Maria Chapdelaine*. Nor should it pass unnoticed that these perceptive lines were written over a decade ago. Yet it is only in the last three or four years that Canadians outside Quebec – and many inside the province, too – have awakened to the fact that the Quebec of Louis Hémon has moved forward to the Quebec of Gabrielle Roy – and beyond.

It is, of course, political events in Quebec that have awakened us, at last, to these changes. But politics in most democratic societies usually fails fully to reflect fundamental shifts in society until long after the most creative writers, artists, and even sociologists have detected these changes. Moreover, there are peculiar reasons why political change has been especially slow in Quebec in the past. What is even more important, however, is that it is the very slow pace at which politics in Quebec – and Ottawa – moved to reflect the basic social transformation which explains the present crisis. And the present crisis is more a crisis within Quebec society itself than a crisis of Confederation. The essence of the crisis, a crisis similar to others that afflict newly emergent nations throughout the world, is that the community's political leaders are attempting to formulate a set of public policies to meet the needs of an urban-industrial society at least a quarter of a century after the society has clearly taken shape. Today, Quebec is a society passing through that characteristic revolution of the mid twentieth century – the revolution of rising expectations, with the expectations ranging from modest demands for increased educational opportunity to demands for total, irrevocable national independence.

Here, then, is the essence of the change that has taken place in Quebec: an agrarian society has been transformed into an urban-industrial one. In this respect Quebec has become more similar to those parts of North America with which it has close geographic relations – Ontario and the north-eastern United States. But this physical transformation has been followed by an equally radical intellectual change: a new view of the role of the state in society has won increasingly wide acceptance. This is so for two reasons. First, in every modern urban-industrial society, the positive role of the state is a fact of life. The state must act to protect workers and their families against the impersonal harshness of an industrial society, to stimulate and often direct the economy, to ensure that the citizens have access to the types of education and training that are necessary in a technological society. No one, except perhaps those whose knowledge of Quebec stops with *Maria Chap-*

delaine, should be surprised that French Canadians, too, have realized the need for this type of public policy. What is surprising is that it took Quebec so long to discover the benefits, and the dangers, of the interventionist state.

Indeed, it is doubly surprising in view of the second reason for the adoption of a new attitude toward the state in Quebec. That second reason rises directly from the dynamic principle of French-Canadian history: *la survivance*. In so far as urbanism and industrialism have made Quebec increasingly similar to its North American neighbours, the dangers of assimilation have likewise increased. The one effective agency over which French Canadians exercise undisputed control, which can be used to counteract the dangers of assimilation inherent in the new society, is the state. This is what Premier Lesage was underlining when he remarked: 'It must be clearly understood that the state of Quebec acts as a fulcrum for the whole French-Canadian community, and at the present time it is the instrument needed for that community's cultural, economic and social progress.'

Again, what is surprising is that it has taken French Canadians so long to face up to the dangers and challenges of industrialism, and to make use of their state creatively. The danger is one that should have been obvious long ago. In 1839 that shrewd analyst Lord Durham argued that assimilation of the French Canadians by the English was desirable because

their present state of rude and equal plenty is fast deteriorating under the pressure of population in the narrow limits to which they are confined. If they attempt to better their condition, by extending themselves over the neighbouring country, they will necessarily get more and more mingled with an English population: if they prefer remaining stationary, the greater part of them must be labourers in the employ of English capitalists. In either case it would appear that the great mass of the French Canadians are doomed, in some measure, to occupy an inferior position, and to be dependent upon the English for employment.

Lord Durham's prediction was a fairly accurate one. The history of Quebec in the latter part of the nineteenth century is the history of a rapidly increasing population. In these years, Quebec had the highest birth-rate in the world, a fact which gave rise to the romantic nationalist notion of *la revanche du berceau*. It was also a community where, by the 1850s, the efficient arable lands were largely occupied. Despite the heroic, but probably misguided, efforts of men like Curé Labelle in the last quarter of the nineteenth century to encourage an effective program of colonization, French Canadians were, in fact, moving more readily in two other directions, both predicted by Durham: about half a million French Canadians emigrated to the United States in the last half of the nineteenth century; then, as the industrial development of the province began to pick up speed, an increasing number of French Canadians became city-dwellers and industrial labourers. Here, briefly, are the figures: in 1901, 40 per cent of the population of Quebec lived in cities; in 1911, the percentage had risen to 48 per cent; another 8 per cent had been added in 1921; the figure was 63 per cent in 1931 and 67 per cent in 1951. And, as Durham had foreseen, both these movements – to the United States and even to the industrial cities of Quebec – threatened the survival of French Canada as a cultural community. But in the long view the industrialization of Quebec will be judged the salvation of the French-Canadian community, for it provided the means whereby the French-Canadian diaspora to the American melting-pot was finally ended. What is new about the 'new Quebec', then, is that French-Canadian leaders have become convinced not only that the French culture can survive in an urban-industrial society but also that that very society, guided by the positive state, can provide a better life than French Canadians have ever experienced. But the critical atmosphere of today's Quebec reflects not only a social transformation but also the recognition by French-Canadian leaders that the new situation contains both potential benefits and potential dangers for the future of French Canada. And it is this tension, a tension inherent in the whole history of French-Canadian nationalism, that underlies the great debates about federalism, autonomism, and separatism; socialism, pragmatism, and conservatism; clericalism and laicism.

Despite the fact that industrialization may now be seen as a means of salvation for French Canadians, it has not always been viewed in such a light. At the end of the eighteenth century, British parliamentary institutions, in a truncated form, were imposed on French Canada in the expectation that they would ultimately encourage the process of assimilation. In fact, French-Canadian leaders soon discovered that these institutions could be used to ensure *la survivance*. By the end of the nineteenth century, industry was being imposed on Quebec, in the sense that it was not a development that French Canadians had asked for or to any large extent participated in at the directing levels. As two economic historians have noted, the 'economic development of Quebec has been financed, directed, and controlled from the outside.' But French Canadians, as in the earlier case of parliamentary institutions, are gradually learning to use the forces of industrial progress to promote and defend *la survivance*.

The process of learning, however, has been a slow one – perhaps almost fatally slow. The reasons for the fears and hostilities with which French Canadians have approached the subject of industrialism have been explored in at least three careful and provocative studies of French-Canadian social thought: by Professor Maurice Tremblay of Laval, and by Pierre-Elliott Trudeau and Professor Michel Brunet, both of the University of Montreal. Although there are important differences in the viewpoints of these writers, they agree on the central argument that the intellectual leaders of French Canada, by virtue of social background, education, religious assumptions, and, not least important, necessity, were for a century or more both blind to the benefits that industrialism could provide and foolish in their repeated praises of the agrarian way of life. In Professor Brunet's words, 'Agriculturalism is above all a general way of thinking, a philosophy of the life which idealizes the past and distrusts the modern social order.' Examples of this ruralist theme are infinite in number, stretching back, as Professor Brunet has shown, nearly to the Conquest, and forward, as M. Trudeau has argued, nearly to the present. One fine example, often overlooked, is Antoine Gérin-Lajoie's novel of 1862. *Jean Rivard: Le Défricheur* sang the praises of the Arcadian way of life and the educated colonizer. Gérin-Lajoie's objective in writing his book was less literary than consciously propagandist. He told his brother quite frankly that his book 'would scarcely amuse the young literary people, but I have composed it with public utility as a goal'. And that goal was to emphasize *la vocation rurale* of French Canada. Indeed, the whole literary school of 1860, as Abbé Casgrain's critical writings make clear, was devoted to the glorification, and deification, of the rural mission.

Such an attitude among literary men is perhaps not wholly unexpected, for the late-flowering influence of the European romantic movement led in an Arcadian direction. It is less understandable, perhaps, in a man who today would probably be described as a social scientist. In his somewhat neglected work *L'Avenir du peuple canadien-*

français, published in 1896, Edmond de Nevers wrote: 'Certainly it cannot be too often repeated, that the most solid basis for a nation is the possession of the land; that the question of "repatriation", that is of the return to the agricultural districts of the province of Quebec, remains the order of the day. Lay hold of the land, as far as circumstances will permit.'

'Emparons-nous du sol, c'est le meilleur moyen de conserver notre nationalité,' became the rallying cry of the agrarian school of nationalists who dominated French-Canadian social thought throughout much of the nineteenth and early twentieth centuries. Jules-Paul Tardivel, the ultramontane separatist editor of *La Vérité*, summed up the position when he wrote in 1902: 'It is not necessary that we possess industry and money. We will no longer be French Canadians but Americans almost like the others. Our mission is to possess the earth and spread ideas. To cling to the soil, to raise large families, to maintain the hearths of intellectual and spiritual life, that must be our role in America.' This was a mission which received the blessing of influential members of the clergy, for the structure of the Church was best adapted to the organization of rural life. Moreover, the rural life placed the French-Canadian Catholic in a position of sharp contrast to the English-speaking Protestant who seemed, in North America, to be more urbanized, more industrialized, more commercialized, and, it was often insisted, more materialistic and thus less Christian. This was the theme of Mgr L.-A. Paquet's famous 'Sermon on the Vocation of the French Race in America', delivered in 1902, the importance of which is perhaps measured by the fact that it was republished in 1925 as *The Breviary of the French Canadian Patriot*. 'Our mission', Mgr Paquet proclaimed, 'is less to manage capital than to stimulate ideas; it consists less in lighting the fires of factories than in maintaining and radiating afar the hearth-light of religion and thought.'

There is, of course, no better or more attractive demonstration of the strength and persistence of the theme of agrarianism than the moving little romance of Maria Chapdelaine written by a French emigré, not a French Canadian, in 1914. Everyone knows the tale of how Maria, having lost her first love, the latter-day *coureur-de-bois* François Paradis, chose to 'dwell on this land as her mother had dwelt and dying thus to leave behind her a sorrowing husband and a record of the virtues of her race' rather than listen to the siren songs of the easy life in a New England mill town. Even better known are the lines:

Three hundred years ago we came and we have remained. . . . Strangers have surrounded us whom it pleases us to call foreigners; they have taken almost all the power; they have taken almost all the wealth; but in Quebec nothing has changed. Nothing will change because we are a pledge. . . . That is why it is necessary to remain in the province where our fathers dwelt, and to live as they lived, so as to obey the unwritten commandment which shaped itself in their hearts, which passed into ours, and which we must transmit in turn to our innumerable children. In the land of Quebec nothing must die and nothing must change.

Undoubtedly Hémon's interpretation of the Quebec he saw was true in the sense that the struggle for survival is unending *au pays du Québec*. Here he struck a universal theme in French-Canadian life. But, even as Hémon was writing, the life of the Chapdelaines of Péribonka was becoming increasingly untypical. Quebec *was* changing; by 1914 about fifty per cent of the people were urban dwellers. A more accurate picture of Quebec, even the Quebec of 1914, had to await the publication in 1938 of Ringuet's brilliant *Thirty Acres*. In it is chronicled the harsh evolution of Quebec rural society and its impact on the shrewd, yet bewildered, Euchariste Moisan. 'The land was failing her own,' Euchariste, in lonely exile in the United States, was forced to conclude; 'the eternal earth-mother would no longer feed her sons.'

The gap between the disintegrating Moisan family farm and the poverty-stricken family of Azarius Lacasse in the slums of the St. Henri district of Montreal is a narrow one. Gabrielle Roy's Florentine Lacasse is mid-twentieth-century Quebec's Maria Chapdelaine. And a reading of *The Tin Flute* makes the fears that many French-Canadian nationalists entertained about the dangers of urbanization and industrialization more understandable. The dangers were undoubtedly present – dangers of poverty, crime, licence, and above all, perhaps, secularization and anglicization. It is the people who lived the lives described by Gabrielle Roy, Roger Lemelin, and Gratien Gélinas, who became determined that a new Quebec must be created where the lives of French-speaking Canadians could be lived more comfortably and securely, economically, socially, and culturally. Gabrielle Roy gives a hint of this new Quebec in the portrayal of the ambitions of Jean Lévesque. 'Have you ever been up on the mountain [Westmount]?' Jean asks Florentine one night. 'You may not think so, my girl, but I expect to get my foot on the first rung of the ladder pretty soon, and then good-bye to St. Henri for me.'

Yet the transformation from the agricultural illusion to a realistic appraisal of the dangers and opportunities of an urban-industrial society is not something that was achieved overnight, and to speak of the total predominance of the rural philosophy is to leave an unbalanced impression of French-Canadian social thought. Some serious and effective criticisms have been directed against those who have neglected another, though less important, side of the picture. Professor F.-A. Angers has suggested that for at least a century there have been scattered voices in Quebec advocating a more positive approach to economic questions. Moreover, Professors Faucher and Lamontagne have effectively argued that 'agricultural expansion coincided with the teachings of a traditional philosophy of rural life; but it cannot be said that it resulted from these teachings: *there was nothing else to do.*' This argument is useful in redressing the balance, but it neither explains the persistence of the agricultural philosophy after there were other things to do, nor does it take into account the people who, even during the period of agricultural expansion, were pointing to the need for more serious consideration of other aspects of Quebec economic life. It is these people who are, in a sense, the real founders of the Quebec of today, and their outlook deserves more consideration and credit than it has been given.

In the mid nineteenth century, just about the time that Gérin-Lajoie was establishing Antoine Rivard as a cultural hero, another thinker was attempting to encourage his fellow-Canadians to turn their attention to what he rightly believed was the wave of the future – industrialism. Etienne Parent, one-time editor of *Le Canadien* and veteran of the political battles of the Papineau period, delivered in 1846 an address entitled 'Industry Considered as the Means of Preserving the French Canadian Nationality'. Industry, Parent told his audience, was the basis of social and political power in North America and the leaders of industry were North America's noblemen. (A later generation was to call them 'robber barons'.) French Canadians had to drop their traditional disdain for business if they wished to conserve their nationality. 'In all branches [of industry and commerce],' he said, 'we are exploited; still we let pass into other hands the riches of our country, and part with the principal element of social power. And the cause of this is that the men we place in competition with those of the other origin are inferior to them in education and capital. Those who could have competed disdain business activity and prefer to vegetate or waste the resources that could have been used to their own profit and that of their country.' If French Canadians refused to pay heed to this warning, Parent continued, a future historian would remark upon the group's disappearance and explain it saying: 'That happened in a country where industry was the only source of wealth and where wealth was the greatest, even the only, means of acquiring social importance. The mass of the people had to be abandoned to the denationalizing influence and action of industrial leaders of the rival race, and so in time lost its national character.' Parent had evidently fully understood the implications of Durham's predictions.

For Parent a revised attitude towards industry and changes in education were necessary if French Canadians were to take their proper place in North American society. And surely here he struck upon an important point that deserves further investigation: that is, the attitude of French Canadians, even French-Canadian businessmen, towards business pursuits, and the scale of social values into which business activity must fit. What work has been done in this field supports the view of an American writer who remarked of France that 'the social order in France has in some measure undervalued the very prizes and penalties that have urged on the capitalist process'. It was this type of situation in Quebec that Parent was attempting to modify, for he recognized that if French Canadians wished to survive in a capitalist and industrial society they must do as the capitalists did.

A recent study of the educational press in nineteenth-century Quebec suggests that Parent was not alone in his concern that commercial education in the province required more emphasis. In 1871 a school of arts and crafts was opened in Quebec City, and the college at Three Rivers began a commercial course. The prospectus of the Collège Masson in 1871 summed up the economic and educational problem of the province in this fashion: 'By raising, with the aid of strong special studies, the industrial and commercial classes to a higher status and to the influence that they have a right and obligation to demand, one can hope that this fortunate foundation will stop the deplorable current which draws almost all our educated young people towards the liberal professions.' And when Laval established courses in applied science in 1871, one newspaper noted: 'Now that the country, and especially our city, has launched itself on the road of manufactures, industry, and railroads, the study of the arts of the applied sciences will be an inappreciable aid to us and will permit us to work a little more for ourselves and by ourselves without being obliged to rely as heavily on assistance from foreigners.'

Further examination of Quebec's educational system in the nineteenth and twentieth centuries will have to be carried out before firm conclusions can be reached about the relation of education to industrialization. It would appear, however, from M. Labarrière-Paulé's study, that by the end of the nineteenth century Quebec educational journals, at least, had become less interested in technical education and more interested in the traditional objectives of French-Canadian clerical nationalism: 'To make the province of Quebec the Christian nation replacing faltering France in the role of the eldest daughter of the Church.' It should be added, however, that this situation reflected more than mere clerical influence. It also reflected the fact that Quebec's economy in the last two decades of the nineteenth century rested in a valley between two peaks of industrial activity – the peak of commercialism and shipbuilding of the 1860s, which had passed, and the peak of industrialism based on electricity, which still lay in the future. In the middle period, about 1870 to 1900, coal, iron, and steam were the characteristic elements of industrial advance, and Quebec lacked them.

By 1900, however, as Quebec arrived at the threshold of a new period of industrial advance, a new apostle of industrialism as a necessary component of French-Canadian survival made his appearance. Errol Bouchette, the very title of whose best-known work, *L'Indépendance économique du Canada français*, illustrates his viewpoint, took up the struggle to interest his countrymen in economic problems where Parent had left off. In 1901 Bouchette warned that the industrial revolution was about to break on Quebec, and that unless preparatory steps were taken, the same problems would be created in Quebec as had been created by the emergence of gigantic trusts in the United States. Foreign capital and business should be welcomed, he noted, but 'we must await them in a good strategic position in order to remain, whenever it happens, *maîtres chez nous*.' Like Parent earlier, Bouchette found it necessary to struggle against the indifference, even the disdain, that his compatriots exhibited towards business. His argument was cast in typically nationalist terms: French Canadians had to become involved in industry, for 'it is to do work not only useful but so essential and obligatory that to fail to do it would be antipatriotic'.

Bouchette, who had no desire to see agriculture disappear from Quebec, realized that not even agriculture could survive if French Canadians lost control of the rest of their economy. Thus he coined, to set alongside the old slogan, 'Emparons-nous du sol', the new one, 'Emparons-nous de l'industrie'. But he did not fool himself that a mere slogan was a panacea for French Canada's industrial weaknesses. First, the educational system of the province had to be adapted to provide education and training in the techniques of commerce and industry. Here he was particularly successful – though he was by no means satisfied – for 1907 witnessed the establishment of commercial schools at both Montreal and Quebec: L'Ecole des Hautes Etudes Commerciales. More important, and more original, was his view that the province needed a carefully worked out industrial policy. 'In order to defend its frontiers [a people] organizes an army,' he wrote; 'if it is a question of constitutional liberty, it organizes a parliament. That is what we have done. It is now a question of protecting our economic life, on which our national existence depends.' And though he disclaimed any sympathy with a socialist viewpoint, he had no doubt that state action was necessary, not least of all because French Canadians, individually, lacked the economic power necessary to cope unassisted with the requirements of an industrial society. 'In a country like ours, where there is so much to do, and rapidly, if we wish to have an absolute guarantee of our survival as a distinct political entity in America,' he wrote, 'reform cannot be carried out without an impulse, direct or indirect, from the collective will of the citizens, that is, by the state.'

The step from Bouchette's point of view to that of René Lévesque is not a long one. The Quebec Minister of Natural Resources stated in the summer of 1963 that 'our principal capitalist for the moment – and as far into the future as we can see – must therefore be the state. It must be more than a participant in the economic development and the emancipation of Quebec; it must be a creative agent.' But although the step is short, it is a difficult one, for it represents the step from advocacy to action, from intellectual analysis to political activity. In the years when Bouchette did his most effective writing, a group of young men in Quebec were attempting to promote similar ideas at the practical political level. Though the founders of La Ligue Nationaliste Canadienne – Olivar Asselin, Jules Fournier, Armand Lavergne, Omer Héroux – are, like their intellectual father Henri Bourassa, most often remembered for their attitude to the British Empire, they also gave considerable thought to domestic economic problems. Indeed, one-third of the league's program was devoted to *politique intérieure*, the two other sections relating to Imperial problems and Dominion-provincial relations. Moreover, the league's newspaper, *Le Nationaliste*, devoted a substantial amount of space to economic questions and to advocating a positive approach to industrial problems. 'The first duty of the French race is to provide itself with a government which thinks for it and which acts for it,' the league's paper maintained.

One of the most interesting statements of the league's philosophy was formulated by the ardent, individualistic Olivar Asselin in a pamphlet published in 1909 under the title *A Quebec View of Canadian Nationalism*. In this lengthy pamphlet Asselin spoke of all aspects of the nationalist program. But the most interesting section is the one dealing with social and economic affairs, which Asselin, somewhat surprisingly, described as 'possibly the most important article in the Nationalists' program'. Here he called for railway nationalization, remarking that 'it is a well-known fact, outside the fool's paradises, that the contest in Ottawa is not so much between Liberals and Conservatives as between this and that combination of railway interests'. The latter remark is interesting not least of all because it is very similar to the view held by western farmers in the same period. Asselin further advocated legislation to ensure conservation of natural resources, public ownership of hydro-electric power, a labour code, social welfare legislation, and stringent control over limited-liability companies and monopolies. Of course, the Nationalists were Canadian and not simply French-Canadian in their viewpoint, but Asselin explained why his group concentrated its attentions on Quebec. 'The National-ists', he wrote, 'have selected Quebec as their first battle-ground precisely because they hoped race hostility would no longer hamper their working for the future greatness of Canada; also because experience has taught them the necessity of educating people to self-government in the smaller spheres first; and thirdly, because they thought that placing the French province of Quebec at the head of Canadian progress should allay the prejudices entertained against the French Canadian as a citizen.'

It is not without interest and significance that Asselin called the Nationalists 'Progressists' in social and econo-mic policy. The name is revealing because the league bears many similarities to the Progressive movement in the United States in the same period: middle-class leadership with its status consciousness, fear of big business but rejec-tion of socialism, emphasis on a non-partisan approach, and, not least of all, nationalism, which in the end proved the league's Achilles' heel. Many of these points were illus-trated in a lecture delivered by Henri Bourassa in Toronto in 1907. 'The Nationalist movement in Quebec', he said, 'is not the movement of a political party.' Having insisted on the Canadianism of the movement, Bourassa then re-marked that 'the Nationalist movement is equally opposed to monopolism and socialism'. But he continued by making it clear that Nationalists believed that the state had an in-creasing role to play in the economic life of Canada and Quebec. It is not surprising that Bourassa showed a sympathetic interest in the developing farmers' movement in the west, which he said was working like the Nationalists 'to save the country from the brutalizing yoke of politicians and plutocrats'. Nor is it surprising that in his later career Bourassa showed some sympathy for the CCF and especially for J. S. Woodsworth. But it would be dangerous to try to make Bourassa (or the Ligue Nationaliste) a consistent social radical. He was, as Laurier said, a *Castor-rouge*, an ultramontane, conservative radical, and in that he was very representative of French-Canadian nationalist thinking.*

By the time the First World War broke out, Bourassa and the league turned their attention increasingly toward more traditional nationalist questions – Imperial policy and minority schools – and the experimental social thinking began to take a poor second place. The events of the war years, especially the Ontario school controversy and conscription, increased the French-Canadian nationalists' tendency to concentrate on traditional policies. The new nationalist spokesmen in the post-war years followed the young historian Abbé Groulx and his *L'Action française*. The organization's writers showed little understanding of, or interest in, economic questions, except perhaps for Olivar Asselin, and its traditionalism was well summed up in an article by Antonio Perrault in 1924:

If we defend our French integrity against imperialism and against assimilative federalism, it is in order to safeguard our Catholic integrity and maintain the apostolic vocation of New France. . . . Without the maintenance of Catholicism, French Canadians would be anglicized; without the conservation of the language and the in-

---

*Bourassa was, to some extent, a typical French-Canadian nationalist in his view of the importance of the agrarian way of life. In 1923 he wrote in *Patriotisme, nationalisme, impérialisme*: 'Our race will survive, grow, and prosper in the measure that it remains peasant and rustic.'

timate springs of the French soul, we would greatly risk ending up as Protestants. Catholicism and French genius, such are the forces from which French Canadians can draw the strength to surmount the obstacles opposed to their survival as a distinct race in America.*

Yet the reformist strain and the positive approach to economic problems never entirely disappeared. Indeed, it was reincarnated in the program of L'Action Libérale Nationale during the depression period, and had it not been for Paul Gouin's political inexperience and Maurice Duplessis's political finesse, public policies more in touch with the needs of the times might have found their way onto the Quebec statute book before the outbreak of the Second World War. But Duplessis swallowed up L'Action Libérale Nationale and in the process the reform program was lost. Only after the long years of Premier Duplessis's ascendency ended in 1959 did the reform forces once more have their opportunity. And by that date the social changes which had taken place in Quebec made reform irresistible.

The reasons for the triumph of the new reform nationalism are multiple. Gradual changes in the educational system created a new class of social critics who dissected society with the tools of twentieth-century social science. Moreover, the educational system began to produce, in rapidly increasing numbers, young people trained to fulfil

---

*In 1921, *L'Action française* devoted its annual 'enquête' to 'notre problème économique'. Two contributors, Edouard Montpetit and Olivar Asselin, tried to keep the discussion on the level of facts and figures. But in his summing up of the discussion Abbé Groulx strongly emphasized the non-material nature of French Canada's mission, almost as though he was afraid that inquiry into material questions might sully the purity of the French-Canadian soul. 'If Catholicism remains for us what it must be,' he wrote, 'if we loyally accept its truth, it indicates to us according to what discipline, in what hierarchy of values, the earthly city ought to be constructed.' (*L'Action française*, Vol. VI, December 1921, page 718)

the requirements of a technological society. Trade union-
ism spread, and behind a militant and dynamic leadership,
working people demanded expanded educational opportunities and effective social legislation. The attitude of the
Church changed, coming increasingly to reflect the altered
society which it served and the liberalizing tendencies of
the world-wide organization to which it belongs. New nations emerged on the world's stage, encouraging French
Canadians to demand a better life for themselves. 'We have
survived enough,' Paul Gérin-Lajoie has written. 'The time
has come to give this survival a positive sense, to fix a goal
for it, and to justify it.'

Somewhere in the hidden recesses of history where sociological changes and intellectual innovations fuse, somewhere around 1959, Quebec began passing through the labour pains that should produce, finally, a more mature,
stable society. And supervising that birth or regeneration is
the newly discovered state of Quebec. 'We must know how
to use this state of ours fearlessly,' Premier Lesage has
said. 'It is not a stranger among us, it belongs to us, and it
proceeds from our people.' But a birth, even with the aid of
such modern medicines as the state provides, is always difficult. And the birth or transformation of a society that uses
the stimulant of nationalism to assist the process is an
especially dangerous affair, for the stimulant may prove
too powerful, thus either slowing up the process or perhaps
even contributing to a stillbirth. There is an inherent tension, perhaps even a contradiction, within the structure of
French-Canadian nationalist thought. That tension, a tension between liberating and reactionary impulses, the
Castor-rouge tension, represents a constant threat to *la survivance* itself.

In a brilliant essay entitled 'La Ligne du risque', Pierre
Vadeboncoeur summed up M. Duplessis's policy in a sen-

tence: 'to resist assimilation from without, to resist emancipation from within'.* Perhaps Vadeboncoeur also, uninten-
tionally, defines here the insoluble dilemma of French Canada: a group of people proud of its traditions, convinced
that survival is its first duty, but condemned to minority
status in North America – condemned to that status whether
as part of the Canadian federal system or separate from
it. The dilemma is found in the fact that the threat of assimilation from outside can only be met by a culturally
and economically strong French Canada; but at the same
time, when energy is used up fighting real or imagined
efforts to assimilate French Canada, there is that much less
energy left to build a strong Quebec.† M. Duplessis, for his

*M. Vadeboncoeur's essay is, in reality, a long indictment of tradi-
tional French-Canadian nationalism – which he sees as reactionary
and conformist – from the viewpoint of an anti-clerical, left-wing
socialist who is also a nationalist. Indeed, the development of M.
Vadeboncoeur's ideas from the position of an anti-nationalist member
of the *Cité libre* group to his present separatist position, a position
which he evidently finds best expressed in the radical separatist
journal *Parti pris*, is an interesting example of one type of evolution
in contemporary Quebec. Whether or not the traditional liberating
ideals of socialism can be made to work in tandem with the conformist
demands of nationalism is a question which M. Vadeboncoeur and
other supporters of Le Parti Socialiste du Québec have attempted to
face but have not yet satisfactorily answered. The order of priority
in the party's aims would seem to place the national before the socialist goals. (See *Le Peuple, Journal du Parti Socialiste du Québec*,
Vol. I, No. 1, September 1963.) The remark in the leading editorial
that 'Socialism has finally begun . . . national liberation will follow'
brings to mind Durham's comment that 'the French appear to have
used their democratic arms for conservative purposes'. (See G. M.
Craig, ed., *Lord Durham's Report*, Toronto, 1963.)

†Of course the separatist argument is that as long as Quebec remains
in Confederation the minority status of French Canadians makes it
impossible to resolve the tension between liberating and reactionary
elements in their nationalism. Therefore they conclude that national
liberation must precede reform. This argument ignores the fact that
French Canadians are a minority because of their geographic posi-

own reasons, followed a policy that drew nearly all of Quebec's energies into the battle for provincial autonomy. But as more and more people awakened to the realization that the battle was a sham, nationalism in Quebec became somewhat discredited; it became, as Gérard Pelletier has written, 'associated with the seamiest side of conservatism and corruption'. And it was during the last years of Duplessis's term of office that reform was reborn, often hostile to, or at least suspicious of, nationalism. But since 1960 nationalism, in a multiplicity of forms, has experienced an enormous revival in Quebec, and in this new situation the old dilemma is once more apparent.

To put the dilemma more concretely: the young reforming intellectuals of La Ligue Nationaliste, despite early professions of interest in economic and social questions, found themselves drawn more and more into struggles for the rights of their group's minority status as Canada passed through the First World War. In the end, their cry for domestic reforms, reforms that would have strengthened the place of French Canadians in the economic life of the country, was lost in the struggle against conscription, against Regulation XVII, against Ottawa, against English Canada. The young reforming intellectuals of L'Action Libérale Nationale were carried away in the same direction by M. Duplessis's war against Ottawa. The brief history of the Bloc Populaire is similarly a witness to the struggle of reaction and reform within a single party. And that conflict within the structure of French-Canadian nationalist thought

---

tion, not because of the British North America Act. For two excellent statements of the separatist position, one historical, the other polemical, see Maurice Séguin, 'Genèse et historique de l'idée séparatiste au Canada français' (*Laurentie*, No. 119, June 1962), and Hubert Aquin, 'L'Existence politique' (*Liberté*, No. 21). For a criticism of the separatist position see Pierre-Elliott Trudeau, 'La Nouvelle Trahison des clercs' (*Cité libre*, April 1962).

is nearly as old as French Canada itself. Papineau faced it, for in his thought and action the traditionalist and the liberal were at war, and the traditionalist won out. It was in this way, as Fernand Ouellet has suggested, that Papineau fulfilled Garneau's description of him as the 'image of our nation'.

It is this very same dilemma that provoked Pierre-Elliott Trudeau to declare, eloquently, in 1961:

Whether or not the Conquest was the origin of all evils and whether or not the English have been the most perfidious occupiers in the memory of man, it remains none the less true that the French-Canadian community holds in its hands, *hic et nunc*, the essential instruments for its regeneration; by the Constitution of Canada the state of Quebec can exercise the most extensive powers over the souls of French Canadians and over the territory where they live – the most rich and most vast of all the Canadian provinces.

Twenty-five years ago, nationalism succeeded in putting to the service of reaction all the energies that had been liberated by the economic crisis of the thirties. It is necessary at any price to prevent the new nationalism from alienating in the same fashion the forces born after the war and which a new unemployment crisis today exacerbates.

Open the frontiers, this people dies of asphyxiation!

Today the dilemma of French Canada remains unchanged. Nationalism can release creative energies in a people; it can also be destructive and reactionary. It can be reactionary because it enforces conformity where individualism and pluralism are necessary if society is to progress. This is the primary danger of the separatist movements and even of the more emotional forms of contemporary French-Canadian nationalism, for both distract the attention of French Canadians from their fundamental problems and turn their energies toward chimeras. M. René Lévesque has remarked: 'If French culture is to spread, if the French language is to be respected, that will depend

above all on the vigour, on the economic and political importance of Quebec.' These goals can be achieved, but they
are endangered by the very dilemma created by nationalism. 'The tasks that we must undertake at any price,' Professor Léon Dion has said, 'the tasks that we must abso-
lutely resolve, are already sufficiently complex and will demand from us sufficient efforts that we should not take to
dreaming of illusory châteaux somewhere other than on the
North American continent.'

The real test of the new Quebec and of the new nationalism is easily summed up: can the tension within French-
Canadian nationalism be resolved? The answer is by no
means clear, but the future not only of Quebec but perhaps
of all Canada is bound up in the resolution of that critical
question.

Every Canadian should welcome the emergence of a new,
self-conscious, democratic Quebec. The successful resolution of the conflicts within the French-Canadian community
depends chiefly on French Canadians themselves, but it also
requires a response from English-speaking Canadians –
a response to the liberating, non-conformist forces in Quebec. By definition, that response must be imaginative and
liberal in character. For English Canadians to ignore the
turmoil within Quebec, or to notice only the extremists demanding the balkanization of our common country, would
be a tragedy. To respond to Quebec's labour pains in dumb
silence or ill-tempered snarls would only strengthen those
reactionary tendencies within French-Canadian ideology.
Today those reactionary forces are more dangerous than
ever, for they could halt a society's natural evolution and
lay up store for a future, perhaps fatal, explosion.

In essence, what the French Canadian is asking for is a
larger, indeed an equal, place for his culture in Canadian

life. More fundamentally, the French Canadian is asking for concrete evidence of the precepts of liberal democracy that Canadians have always claimed provide the basis of their political life. And the French Canadian's yardstick of Canadian liberalism is the yardstick described many years ago by the English historian Lord Acton, when he wrote: 'The co-existence of several nations under the same state is the test, as well as the best guarantee, of freedom.'

Today many French Canadians believe that English Canadians must assist in bringing reality into closer conformity with that ideal. The challenge of the new Quebec is really a challenge to Canada. And that challenge is summed up in one of the most pressing questions that the country must face in the sixties: can two cultural communities that have as much in common as French and English Canada work out a fruitful partnership within the bosom of a single state? Such a partnership must promote the values of liberty and individual self-fulfilment, and these values must take precedence over the conformist demands of nationalism, English- or French-Canadian. Can we devise the terms of a partnership that will measure up to Lord Acton's yardstick? In a world divided by national boundaries, ideological quarrels, and economic inequalities, but united by the potential benefits and dangers of modern technology, the answer to that Canadian question has a significance that transcends the borders of the Canadian community.*

*For a greatly expanded and much more specific statement of some of the generalities expressed in these last few paragraphs, see the important article by Pierre-Elliott Trudeau *et al.*, 'An Appeal for Realism in Politics', *Canadian Forum*, Vol. XLIV, No. 520, May 1964.

SIX

In the Bourassa Tradition

One argument in favour of bilingualism in Canada is that English Canadians who do not at least read French miss a great deal of vigorous writing in all fields — literature, politics, sociology, and religion. Moreover, they miss the opportunity of reading the most intellectual newspaper in Canada, *Le Devoir*. No English Canadian who has read this serious-minded Montreal daily at any time since its foundation in 1910 by Henri Bourassa can feel anything but regret that we have nothing to compare with it in English Canada. And the most impressive feature of the newspaper has always been its editorial page. It is, of course, a *nationaliste* newspaper and every editorial writer from Bourassa and Omer Héroux, through Georges Pelletier, to André Laurendeau at the present time, has been deeply committed to the cause of *la survivance*. But *Le Devoir* has always been concerned with more than just the negative defence of the rights of *la nation canadienne-française* (though this is the side that English Canadians have usually noticed). Equally important has been its role as the constant critic of life in Quebec. It has fought for higher educational standards, for the purity of the French language, for the rights of trade unions, for social security, and, perhaps above all (because it precedes all these), public morality. For example, in the late fifties it fought Premier Duplessis so vigorously that 'Le Chef' excluded the parliamentary correspondent of *Le Devoir* from his press conferences. The correspondent, M. Pierre Laporte, is today a leading member of the Lesage government.

Le Devoir has stood for the kind of things that make a newspaper great and that give it what J. W. Dafoe once called 'personality'. Probably the most important reason for *Le Devoir*'s consistently high quality has been the series of men who have guided it through fifty years' fighting. Henri Bourassa, one of the most impressively intellectual figures in our history, set the standard. Bourassa wanted a journal that would break with the traditional servile party press in Quebec, a paper whose 'duty' would be to defend the rights of French Canadians throughout Canada, the autonomy of Quebec within the federal system, and the autonomy of Canada within the British Empire. Independence from party, but commitment to the religious, political, and cultural interests of French Canada, were Bourassa's watchwords. Today the interpretation and application of those watchwords is the responsibility of a man who, thanks largely to the CBC, is not unknown in English Canada. It is not so many years since the radio program 'Weekend Review' regularly brought to English Canada the gentle accent, penetrating analysis, and unique style of André Laurendeau.

Probably there were few of M. Laurendeau's listeners who were aware of his varied and controversial background. Indeed there would certainly have been some English Canadians who would have abruptly turned off the radio and hoisted the Union Jack had they realized that at various times since 1935 M. Laurendeau had been a separatist, a neutralist, an editor of *L'Action nationale*, a leader of La Ligue pour la Défense du Canada which campaigned against conscription during the Second World War, a founder of the Bloc Populaire, and a one-time Bloc member of the Quebec legislature. In 1944 Blair Fraser told his readers, 'Laurendeau is a man to watch in Quebec politics. A fanatic nationalist, a rabble-rousing speaker, yet a cool, calculating mind . . . . ' In all of his varied activities, M. Laurendeau has attempted to give expression to views that are those of a 'nationalist' and a 'socially conscious Christian'.

But to describe M. Laurendeau as a nationalist is to say very little. Nearly every French Canadian is a nationalist if that amorphous term is taken to mean a belief in French Canada's right to survive as a cultural group. Laurier, Bourassa, Canon Groulx, Duplessis, and Marcel Chaput, to name only a few, are all people who could be fitted into a definition of nationalism. But what these people have in common is probably less significant than their differences. M. Laurendeau, although he shares some qualities with each of them, has gradually evolved his own position. That position contains far more of Henri Bourassa and Canon Groulx than of Laurier or Marcel Chaput.

M. Laurendeau was born into a family that was steeped in the Bourassa tradition. Henri Bourassa's thinking developed in the years between the Boer War and the First World War when the power of the British Empire still seemed to be at its height. He fought hard to convince Canadians that their future lay neither in continuing as a colony with no voice in the determination of Canadian foreign policy, nor in closer integration into an Empire that would speak with a common, co-operative voice in foreign affairs. Bourassa believed that Canada should become a sovereign nation in her own right, within the British family of nations, but with full control over every aspect of her own affairs. He also believed that Canada should be a particular kind of nation formed on the basis of an equal partnership between French and English. One of his greatest fears, a fear shared by Sir Wilfrid Laurier, was that Canadian involvement in Imperial affairs would divide French and English Canadians along cultural lines. In 1902 he set forth his mature thoughts about Canada when he remarked:

A mutual regard for racial sympathies on both sides, and a proper discharge of our exclusive duty to this land of ours, such is the only ground upon which it is possible for us to meet so as to work out our national problems. There are here neither masters nor valets; there are neither conquerors nor conquered ones; there are two partners whose partnership was entered into upon fair and well-defined lines. We do not ask that our English-speaking fellow-countrymen should help us to draw closer to France; but, on the other hand, they have no right to take advantage of their overwhelming majority to infringe on the treaty of alliance, and induce us to assume, however freely and spontaneously, additional burdens in defence of Great Britain.

As pressure for Canadian involvement in Imperial and world affairs increased, and as the rights of the French-speaking minorities outside Quebec were gradually whittled away, Bourassa's dream of a bicultural nation seemed to grow less and less attainable. Though Bourassa lived to see his country involved in the Second World War, the peak of his political career was passed by the 1920s.

To many young French Canadians growing up in the late twenties and early thirties, Bourassa was a figure to be respected, but also one who was viewed as something of an exhausted volcano. In his brilliant essay 'Le Nationalisme de Bourassa', M. Laurendeau described his own youthful doubts about the old nationalist chief who had once seemed a true tribune of his people, but who was now either silent, or, worse, openly condemning extreme nationalism. In these same years a new intellectual leader had made his appearance on the Quebec scene, and he was giving nationalism a new, more radical turn. He was Abbé Lionel Groulx, a professor of history. Unlike many French-Canadian historians, Groulx was more interested in what had happened to French Canadians after the British Conquest than he was in painting portraits of the Golden Age of New France, though he did that too. Moreover, he used history to illustrate the unique, unchangeable qualities of French Canadians, a uniqueness he described by the word 'race'. His early books all emphasized the view implied in titles like *L'Appel de la race* and *La Naissance d'une race*. One is inevitably unfair to Abbé Groulx in summarizing his ideas, but his general conception was one that emphasized the rather mystical separateness of French Canadians; his nationalism was characterized by a strongly religious and messianic flavour. Where Bourassa had spoken of a broad Canadianism based on cultural duality, Groulx insisted on French Canadianism, and warned against siren songs of Canadianism. In the early twenties he wrote:

The future and Providence are going to work for us. Joseph de Maistre wrote on the morrow of the French Revolution that God had made such a terrible clean sweep only to lay bare the basis for the future. Let us believe with firm faith that after the vast disorder of the Great War there will be room for marvellous constructions. We make only this prayer to our leaders and to all the chiefs of our race: know how to foresee and to act. Grant that they may no more abandon the development of our life to improvisation and to incoherent action; that for the vanity of a too largely Canadian patriotism they may not sacrifice us to the dream of an impossible unity; that they may know how to reserve the future; that before concluding and deciding our destinies they may take account of the premises of our history; and God will not let perish that which he has conserved by so many miracles.

Abbé Groulx's national doctrine was strongly separatist in its implications. In the twenties, like many other Canadians, he believed that Confederation was falling apart and he hoped to see the establishment of a French and Catholic state on the banks of the St. Lawrence. By the thirties, this dream had slipped into the background. And once the depression came the Abbé's social views began to attract some support. Essentially these views took the form of the traditional conservative nationalist's glorification of the agrarian way of life. But during the depression his remarks took on an anti-capitalist tenor that struck a sympathetic note for the new generation of young, urban intellectuals who all around them witnessed economic stagnation and social dislocation. Groulx's views, especially on economic questions, appealed to young nationalists who saw that the economic transformation of Quebec was taking place under the control of English-Canadian, British, and American capitalists. Here was a transformation that was virtually a new conquest. In 1936 Abbé Groulx declared that because of foreign domination of the Quebec economy, 'with our own property, with our own work, with our own savings we build our economic servitude'.

It was Groulx's teachings that inspired the Jeune-Canada movement. And André Laurendeau, at twenty-four, expressed the sentiments of the movement in a lyrical separatist tract entitled *Notre nationalisme* which he published in October 1935. 'Laurentie reigns over me,' he declared, 'not as a tyrant of which I would be a slave! Rather as an ideal freely chosen and passionately served!' Young Laurendeau's dedication of the pamphlet was a shrewd self-analysis of the influence and weight that he gave to his intellectual seniors: 'To Henri Bourassa and Abbé Groulx, the one a precursor, the other the craftsman of the doctrine from which these pages proceed.'

The influence of the 'craftsman' Abbé Groulx was deeply imprinted on Laurendeau when he left to continue his

studies in France in 1935. At the Sorbonne he discovered a
new kind of Christian and humanitarian influence in the
teachings of Jacques Maritain, Nicholas Berdiaeff, and
Emmanuel Mounier. In addition, the writings of Malraux,
Bernanos, and Dostoievski were opened up to him. And in
the Europe of the mid thirties no one as intelligent and sensitive as André Laurendeau could miss observing the
dangers of racism in its Nazi and Fascist forms. In his book
La Crise de la conscription – 1942, published in 1962, M.
Laurendeau wrote of these days in France: 'When the war
in Spain broke out my sympathies did not go to Franco
. . . at the same time I felt myself more and more opposed
to the Fascist régime, especially Naziism; for I discovered
the demands and the greatness of a democracy purged of
capitalist poison.' Clearly the conservative social teachings
of Abbé Groulx were giving way under the impact of the
French Catholic left. In a letter from Paris to *L'Action
nationale* in January 1937 he remarked that 'God is not a
bourgeois policeman charged with defending the great
properties of nobles and of certain religious communities,
and the shameful expropriation of the poor by the large
capitalists . . . .'

It was also in France that M. Laurendeau began to learn
of the Canada that existed beyond the borders of the province of Quebec. He learned from the famous French Protestant sociologist and historian André Siegfried, at the
Collège de France. Siegfried had long been a student of Canada and his book *The Race Question in Canada*, published
in 1907, was one of the most penetrating analyses of Canadian society ever written. Strangely, it was this French-
man who set Laurendeau to thinking about the people with
whom he lived without knowing in Canada. Clearly, when
he returned to Montreal his mind had been opened to a
wider Canada and a wider world.

The Canada he returned to in 1937, and especially the Quebec, was increasingly uneasy about the way of the world. War in Europe seemed inevitable, and for French Canadians the memory of 1917 and conscription was never far below the surface. It was in this atmosphere that the twenty-seven-year-old student turned to journalism, assuming the editorship of the province's most influential nationalist magazine, *L'Action nationale*. Once again his attention was turned to *la survivance*. But Europe had made its mark and Laurendeau wanted it clearly understood that racism had no place in the nationalist movement. Intellectual stimulus still came from the same source as before, as his pamphlet *L'Abbé Lionel Groulx* in the series 'Nos maîtres de l'heure', published in January 1939, made clear. Yet he had determined on returning from France to pursue the interests opened up by Siegfried. He enrolled at McGill in an effort to make contact with English Canadians of his own age. Soon he discovered a left-wing group that seemed to share his anti-imperialism, and by the spring of 1939 he had formed a close association with these students. At this point, he wrote later, 'we dared even to speak of a Canadian nation'. But the university vacation arrived and at the end of the long summer of 1939 came the outbreak of war. Now it became apparent that the assumptions of the French- and English-Canadian student friends had been radically different. The English Canadians, though often reluctantly, chose to support the decision that took Canada into the war. Laurendeau did not. He recalled the repeated promises of the Liberals in Quebec that Canada would not again be involved in a British war. And this was just what the 1939 war seemed to be. Like Bourassa in his opposition to Canadian participation in the Boer War, Laurendeau expressed the deep-felt frustration of finding himself at odds with the majority's commitment to what he was sure was a war that did not directly involve Canadian interests. Surely this was proof of Canada's continuing colonialism. 'In theory,' he recalled later, 'we have been free since the Statute of Westminster; in practice, through the will of the Anglo-Canadians, we cease to be free on important occasions.'

Like so many other French Canadians brought up in the nationalist tradition, Laurendeau believed that the first line of defence for French Canadians was in Quebec. Above all, the province's autonomy must be guarded against the inevitable centralizing temptations that the war effort would present to Ottawa. In a pamphlet published shortly after the outbreak of the war and entitled *Alerte aux Canadiens-français*, he called his compatriots to arms in the defence of their province's autonomy. 'Here we will defend provincial autonomy, the Confederation placed in peril by the centralizing faction, and the existence of French Canada.'

In his little semi-autobiographical study of the war years, *La Crise de la conscription*, M. Laurendeau gives a full and frank account of his efforts to prevent the central government from using the power that above all reminds the French Canadian of his minority status – the power of military conscription for overseas service. Carefully he watched the King government, with its strong Quebec base, retreat from one position after another as it moved slowly but surely towards conscription: from pre-war promises of non-participation to limited participation, from limited participation to full-scale mobilization for overseas service, from conscription for home service to the point in 1942 when Prime Minister King decided to ask the country to release his government from its pledge never to adopt a policy of conscription for overseas service. What annoyed French-Canadian nationalists most about the 1942 plebiscite proposal was that they believed that a bargain or contract had been made in 1939 in Ernest Lapointe's famous pledge to oppose conscription, that the pledge had been renewed in the Quebec provincial election of 1939 which saw Maurice Duplessis defeated, and that for a third time in the federal election of 1940 the promise had been made, whereby French Canadians agreed to support the war on the understanding that participation by individuals would remain voluntary. But in 1942 the whole of Canada, and not just French Canada to whom the pledge had been made, was asked to release the government from its contract. M. Laurendeau and his friends determined to fight against the revocation of the no-conscription pledge.

It is the fight for a negative answer on the plebiscite that M. Laurendeau describes in *La Crise de la conscription*. It is not objective history, but rather an honest attempt to recall the emotions and opinions of the war years. Yet despite the emotion and depth of the crisis, the book is without malevolence or hatred. (How many English Canadians who fought for an affirmative answer in 1942 could say the same of their recollections?) But the central point of the book cannot be missed. M. Laurendeau writes:

During the war many Quebec French Canadians felt that they were living in an occupied country. The English occupied it, it was they who dictated its conduct and prevented the national will from expressing itself effectively; our politicians were collaborators. It was, in comparison to Hitler's Europe, a benign occupation; thanks to King's moderation, the weight was supportable. We risked only our liberties; yet the menace was only occasionally fulfilled. But its existence was enough to poison life.

Despite this feeling of occupation, it is worth emphasizing, a group that formed itself into an organization to fight the plebiscite adopted the title of 'The League for the Defence of Canada' (not French Canada). Though M. Laurendeau does not make much of this point in his book, a re-reading of the league's manifesto would no doubt have reminded him of the strength of the group's belief that their cause reached out beyond the French-Canadian community. The final paragraph of that appeal read:

It is thus not as a province nor as an ethnic group that we take our position. If we refuse to release the government from its engagements of 1939 and 1940, we do it as citizens of Canada, placing above everything the interests of Canada. There exists in this country, we believe, a majority of Canadians for which Canada is the fatherland, and for whom the slogan 'Canada d'abord' or 'Canada first' has never been a simple electoral cry, but the expression of a profound sentiment and of a supreme spiritual conviction. We make our appeal to all those people. We ask them to put their country above the spirit of race or of partisan considerations. Do they wish to take an action that will stop the movement towards the abyss, and which will forcefully attest a majority voice from one ocean to another? To Mr. King's plebiscite, with all the calmness and force of free men, they will reply with a resounding no.

God save our country! Long live Canada!

But La Ligue pour la Défense du Canada found little support among English-speaking Canadians, most of whom were convinced that the defeat of Hitler and his allies was the prime interest of Canada. Nevertheless, M. Laurendeau and his friends carried on a vigorous battle despite such obstacles as the refusal of the CBC (on grounds of neutrality) to allow the forces favouring a negative answer to the plebiscite to use the publicly-owned network. When the vote was counted, seventy-one per cent of the Quebec vote was negative, and if the English-Canadian voters in Quebec are subtracted from the provincial total, the French-Canadian 'non' had ninety per cent approval.

Quebec was isolated once more. M. Laurendeau and his friends turned their temporary organization into something more permanent and founded a new nationalist party, the

Bloc Populaire. For these men, the old parties were completely discredited and none of the 'new parties', the CCF, the Social Credit, or even the Union Nationale whose leader had betrayed his early reformist allies, was acceptable. M. Laurendeau became secretary of the Bloc, and sat briefly in the Quebec legislature. But the party never achieved any widespread appeal, and soon it found itself divided between its more traditionalist, conservative nationalist supporters and a more radical, almost socialist wing. The latter was M. Laurendeau's wing. Soon M. Duplessis had provided a home for the conservative elements, while M. St. Laurent and prosperity removed many French-Canadian grievances and healed old wounds. M. Laurendeau, never happy in politics, returned to journalism. It was, of course, nationalist journalism, with *L'Action nationale* and *Le Devoir*.

But his nationalism was never narrow or fanatical. It was constantly being subjected to self-criticism. Nor, even after the experience of the war years, was he ever seriously tempted to return to his youthful separatist fantasies. Indeed, as he began to travel throughout Canada to talk to English Canadians on CBC radio, and, perhaps most important, as he began to look once more to the outside world with its changing balance of power and its threatening cold war, his vision of Canada broadened again. In a series of articles written for *L'Action nationale* in 1952 and entitled 'Y a-t-il une crise du nationalisme?' he perceptively explored this changed world and Canada's place in it. He found that while the power of both Britain and France had declined, the United States had grown to the status of a super-power. Like so many Canadian nationalists, French and English, he realized that the old battles for Canadian autonomy offered little guidance for a future in which the United States, not Britain, was the threat to Canadian sur-

vival. Like all French-Canadian nationalists of the Bourassa school, M. Laurendeau was deeply aware that the
power of the United States represented a greater potential
threat to French Canadians divided from the rest of Canada
than to French Canadians allied to the rest of Canada.
French Canadians, while defending their culture and the
autonomy of Quebec, would find more security in attempting to forge a new alliance with English Canada than in
turning their backs blindly to the outside world.

Throughout the fifties M. Laurendeau was a stout defender of his province's autonomy against the growing
power of an Ottawa spurred on by a confident new Canadianism. He was doubtless a little embarrassed in defending the autonomy of the province when he had so little
sympathy with the policies of the apparently invincible
ruling party, the Union Nationale. Still, by the end of the
fifties the province began to develop a new spirit and new
energy. The death of Maurice Duplessis in 1959 marked
the end of the ice-age in Quebec politics. The very fact that
Duplessis's successor, Paul Sauvé, was a reformer indicated that the old order had passed. But neither the brief
Sauvé administration nor its successor, the Lesage Liberal
régime, has been entirely able to define clearly the shape
of the future. But one thing is clear: many of the reforms
in public life, in education, and in economic development
found echoes in the columns of *Le Devoir* under M.
Laurendeau's guidance.

With the birth of reform in the new Quebec has come
much turbulence and discontent, which, as always, ex-
presses itself in the language of nationalism. Once more
a separatist movement has been born, stronger and more
effectively organized than at any time since 1837 and, on
the fringes, talking the same language of totalitarianism
and violence that has characterized young nationalist

movements in countries suffering the worst excesses of European imperialism. The battle of the sixties, then, is not merely the old one of *la survivance* fought with new weapons, but also a dispute about the future shape of Canada. The main scene of the struggle is in Quebec itself, for, in M. Laurendeau's view, 'at Quebec one does what one wishes; at Ottawa one does what one can'. The French Canadians are a majority in Quebec and there they can decide and implement the changes that are necessary in their society. But they are an important minority in all Canada and they must do what they can to make that position more secure. M. Laurendeau is not a separatist; indeed, he presents the young separatist with the most effective counter-arguments. He is not a separatist because he is a realist. More important, he has grown more and more to appreciate the values of his original mentor, Henri Bourassa. In 1904 Bourassa had a public exchange with J. P. Tardivel, whose journal *La Vérité*, devoted exclusively to the development of French-Canadian nationalism, criticized Bourassa for his 'Canadianism'. Bourassa's reply was unequivocal:

The fatherland, for us, is the whole of Canada, that is to say, a federation of distinct races and autonomous provinces. The nation that we wish to see developed is the Canadian nation, composed of French Canadians and English Canadians, that is to say, two elements separated by language and religion, and by the legal arrangements necessary for the conservation of their respective traditions, but united in an attachment of brotherhood, in a common attachment to a common fatherland.

Essentially this is M. Laurendeau's position. French and English Canadians must stand together if their common 'fatherland' is to have a future. But he hopes that they will stand together in the Bourassa tradition of mutual respect and equality of rights for French- and English-speaking Canadians from coast to coast. That is why he so frequently called for a positive response from English Canada to the new currents that are running through Quebec society. That is why he advocated the appointment of a royal commission to examine the existing relationships between French and English Canadians. Now that he is co-chairman of that commission the same qualities of understanding and courage, of intellectual clarity and humane urbanity that have characterized his life will ensure an investigation and a report of the most thorough and searching kind.

The *Preliminary Report of the Royal Commission on Bilingualism and Biculturalism* contains many sections that bear the clear Laurendeau imprint. None sums up better the intellectual honesty that lies at the heart of the Bourassa tradition than these lines from the document's preamble: '. . . the feeling of the Commission is that at this point the danger of a clear and frank statement is less than the danger of silence; this type of disease cannot be cured by keeping it hidden indefinitely from the patient.'

At the end of his essay on Bourassa, M. Laurendeau recalls a remark made to him by an English Canadian: 'The point about Bourassa is that he does not belong to French Canada alone.' It is time that the same remark was made about André Laurendeau. For the editor-in-chief of *Le Devoir* there is no distinction, except Bourassa's distinction, between *Canadien* and Canadian.

SEVEN

The Historian and Nationalism

English Canadians have an underdeveloped historical consciousness. Neither on the popular nor on the intellectual
level does history deeply affect our lives and thoughts. We
have no myths and no successful myth-makers. This is
merely another way of saying that English-Canadian
nationalism is immature, for a consciousness of the past
is the stuff out of which nationalism is made. It is no accident that the first Western people with a historical consciousness is also the people whose history provides the
archetype of modern nationalism: the Jewish people. Nor
is it an accident that, unlike most Western peoples, English
Canadians lack a 'national historian', a Bancroft or a
Macaulay. This does not mean that our historians have not
been nationalists. On the contrary, nearly all of them have
been. But none has found the interpretation of our history
that can be called *the* national interpretation, though nearly
all play some variation on the theme of survival against
the threats of the United States.*

*That A. R. M. Lower's *Colony to Nation* (Toronto, 1946) and D. G.
Creighton's *Dominion of the North* (Toronto, 1945) are both expressions of Canadian nationalism is obvious. But the difference of
viewpoint is almost equally obvious.

Whatever nationalism there is in English Canada is based not only on the survival theme but also on the British Conquest in 1760. That event gave English Canadians one very necessary component of nationalism: a sense of superiority. Yet the Conquest has not been presented as a great national event by our historians, probably because it divides Canadians. Also, of course, in the democratic twentieth century, conquest cannot really be unashamedly celebrated. Therefore, English Canadians have usually rationalized the Conquest by insisting that it brought French Canada the blessings of English liberty. The very ambivalence of English Canadians on the subject of the Conquest is an example of an anaemic nationalism. ·

The explanation of English Canada's lack of a historical consciousness is simple. Our orderly growth from 'colony to nation' has deprived us of the heroic events out of which nationalist myths are made. There is no great, romantic, uniting theme – a revolution or a defence of the fatherland – on which to build a national doctrine. What heroes there are are nearly all French, thus making English-Canadian hero-worship difficult. There is no English-Canadian Dollard or Brébeuf, and most English Canadians are unable to read the language in which these myths are expressed. Only John A. Macdonald comes near to being a national hero of mythical stature, but he is too real to qualify fully. Politicians rarely do, and if they do, it is only because, somehow, they are able to rise above politics; George Washington is a good example. Finally, English Canadians have always been rather uninterested in the past because of their preoccupation with building the present and ensuring the future. While some societies realize the usefulness of historical myths and of national pride in building a nation, English Canadians – perhaps content to live vicariously on others' myths – have been more concerned with railways, tariffs, and settlement. Nationalism is rarely spawned by the prosaic and the practical.

The lack of an inspiring national history in English Canada becomes particularly clear when a contrast is drawn with French Canada. Nationalism and historical writing have always been intimately linked in French Canada. This is only natural for a society that has all the elements of a national mythology in its past: heroes and heroines, wars and adventures, herculean struggles against man and nature, the ultimate tragedy of the British Conquest, and, above all, the sense of mission that all these events combine to foster. With this backdrop, it is little wonder that historians in French Canada have played perhaps the largest single role in developing the nationalist ideology.

The first great French-Canadian historian, the first national historian, was François-Xavier Garneau. Garneau composed his magnificent *Histoire du Canada depuis sa découverte jusqu'à nos jours*, which began to appear in 1845, to refute Durham's claim that French Canadians lacked both history and literature. The *Histoire* disposed of both charges effectively, and in its depiction of the glories of *la survivance* fulfilled yet another purpose. 'I wish', Garneau revealed to L.-H. Lafontaine, 'to imprint this nationality with a character which will make it respected by the future.'

Garneau's drum-and-trumpet account of the history of his nation dominated French-Canadian historical writing for over half a century. In its later editions, it was emasculated of most of the remarks that had left its author open to the suspicion of anti-clericalism and secularism. Thus, though French Canada's first national historian was a layman, the liberal interpretation that he gave to his people's past was soon transformed by the more conservative and clerical nationalism that triumphed in Quebec during the last third of the nineteenth century. Here French Canada, as it often does, was reflecting developments in Europe, where the liberal nationalism of 1848 was falling victim to the conservative, Bismarckian type, while the liberal Pius IX was transforming himself into the reactionary Pius IX. Though Garneau had many successors – not the least of whom was the Abbé Ferland – no one immediately replaced him on the pedestal of national historian. Moreover, from the 1870s until the First World War, it was more often clerics like Bishop Laflèche and Mgr L.-A. Paquet who provided the theoretical framework and moral exhortation for French-Canadian nationalists. It is not surprising that the greatest nationalist to emerge in this period was a man whose loyalty to his people was exceeded only by his loyalty to his church: Henri Bourassa.

While Bourassa was not an historian, he recognized the importance of history in the struggle for survival. It was partly as a result of his campaign in *Le Devoir* that, for the first time since 1865, professors of history were appointed in 1915 at both branches of Laval University. The chair at Quebec went to the temperamentally and politically conservative Thomas Chapais. His great *Cours d'histoire du Canada* will stand for many years as a model of careful, well-documented political and constitutional history. But Chapais, because of his location in Quebec City, or his temperamental conservatism, or his political realism, or his enormous respect for documents and facts, never developed an all-encompassing 'national doctrine' with which to explain his people's past and present. That task he left to his colleague in the Chair of History at Montreal.*

*Comparing Chapais and Groulx, Olivar Asselin wrote that 'the English of Chapais were men we have never seen except in books; those

Abbé Lionel Groulx was, and indeed still is, the real successor to Garneau. The first fact about him, obvious but profoundly important, was his clerical training. No trace of the liberal scepticism that had marked Garneau's early work was allowed to creep into his writing. His education in Canada and in Europe came when both religious and nationalist thought were conservative. He reached his maturity and cut his political teeth during the years when the bicultural Canadian nationalism preached by Bourassa was meeting its most serious setbacks in the school and conscription crises. Perhaps the most revealing of all Abbé Groulx's books is the now-almost-forgotten novel he wrote under a pseudonym, *L'Appel de la race*. The novel took as its background the struggle against the famous Ontario School Regulation XVII and had as its central theme a *vendu*'s recovery of his French Canadianism and the consequent loss of his English-Canadian wife. It is hard to avoid the separatist implications in this Canadian 'mixed marriage'. While Groulx's disciples and admirers have insisted that his use of the word 'race' had little significance, a reading of his novel suggests otherwise. The young historian was doubtless not a member of the racist school of Gobineau and H. S. Chamberlain, but his belief in French-Canadian uniqueness meant that his use of 'race' implied profound and unchangeable characteristics.

In a sense there were two Abbé Groulxs. One was the careful historian whose career was crowned by his *Histoire du Canada français*, in which the glories of survival were celebrated in a fashion both scholarly and lyrical. The other was the speaker, publicist, and pamphleteer, editor of *L'Action française* in the twenties and intellectual men-

---

of Groulx with their Jekyll and Hyde double personality are those that we have known since our childhood.' (Cited in Mason Wade, *The French Canadians, 1760-1945*, Toronto, 1954, page 875.)

tor of *L'Action nationale* in the thirties and forties. The two roles were never completely distinct. In the essays he collected under the revealing title *Notre maître, le passé*, he used his historical studies to expound his nationalist doctrine. And this doctrine always was that for French Canadians, French Canada came first. French Canada might, he seemed to suggest in the twenties, gradually regain its independence. Or it might, as he later seemed resigned to conclude, remain an autonomous part of a larger Canada. But French Canadians would survive only if they gave their first, indeed only, emotional loyalty to French Canada. It was here that Groulx sought to shift the balance, always delicately poised in Bourassa's thought, toward French Canada. Groulx, in fact, harked back to the tradition of the ultramontane separatist of the late nineteenth century, Jules-Paul Tardivel, with whom Bourassa had debated over the relative merits of Canadian and French-Canadian nationalism. Groulx, like Tardivel but unlike the complex Bourassa, was a French-Canadian, not a Canadian, nationalist.

History, in Groulx's view, was the story of *la survivance*. But more philosophically, it was a play in which two actors participated: man and God. 'The more perfect the collaboration between these two, the greater the history.' Groulx's examination of the heroic days of New France convinced him that the collaboration was close indeed and that French Canadians were *une race élue*, 'a chosen race'. The purpose of an awareness of history was explicitly nationalist. 'To reveal the very close identity of blood and its perfect purity, to fasten upon then indicate the moral traits of the race, that is the work of our history, which, in this way, establishes more solidly among us the very foundation of nationality.'

The past was glorious and provided stimulus and motivation in a difficult present. The French-Canadian past was a success story because the people had remained faithful to their religion and their nationality.

Of all the figures of the past whom Groulx set forth as examples for French Canadians to emulate, none took precedence over Dollard, the hero of the Long Sault. In Groulx's view, Dollard epitomized the union of Catholicism and the French tradition that was French-Canadian nationalism. In 1919, Groulx concluded an impassioned speech entitled 'Si Dollard revenait...' with the ringing exhortation:

Rise, then, O Dollard, living on your granite pedestal. Call us with your manly charm and in your heroic accents. We will rise towards you with hands trembling like palms, ardently desiring to serve. Together we will work, we will rebuild the family house. And for the defence of our Frenchness and of our Catholicism, if you so command, O Dollard, rapturous and magnetic leader, we will follow you to the final holocaust.

The religious, messianic tone of this incantation need hardly be underlined. Where religious conviction nearly always took clear precedence over nationalist ideals (though the two were closely related) in Bourassa, it would be difficult to make this distinction in Groulx's thought. And it was the inseparable combination of these elements that he regarded as the essence of French-Canadian history and nationalism.*

While Canon Groulx lives and writes, no French Canadian can aspire to replace him as 'national historian', even though his religiously oriented nationalism grows increasingly anachronistic in the new atmosphere of Quebec. Moreover, among his successors, history has become a discipline, at least at first glance, more subject to scientific

---

*For a brilliant analysis of the nationalism of the Groulx school, see Maurice Tremblay, 'Réflexions sur le nationalisme', *Ecrits du Canada français*, Vol. V, 1959, pages 9-45.

investigation and more interesting for its own sake than
for the precepts it teaches for today's battles. At first
glance, perhaps; but in actual fact the tradition of history
as a fundamental of *la survivance* and nationalist doctrine
remains as strong as ever. Much first-class history has been
written, and will continue to be written, by men like Marcel
Trudel, Guy Frégault, and Michel Brunet, as well as other
younger men. Nevertheless, as long as French Canadians
remain a cohesive, national community, proud of their past
but insecure in a present dominated by the non-French
majority in North America, nationalists will continue to
search the past for the weapons of survival. The best contemporary example is Professor Michel Brunet, director
of l'Institut d'Histoire of the University of Montreal.

In some superficial ways, Brunet resembles Canon
Groulx. He combines research into the past with an enormous interest in the problems of present-day Quebec. He
is nearly as interested in public education as he is in his
university career. His warmth and wit, as well as certain
other qualities, make him one of Quebec's most popular
intellectuals. There is a danger in this type of popularity
from which Brunet has not entirely escaped: the simplifi-
cation of subtle ideas. But the points of similarity with
Canon Groulx end when Brunet's lay status is noted. 'It is
impossible to understand the new nationalists if one does
not first see them as lay historians; similarly, one cannot
understand Groulx if one does not recognize, behind the
writer, the cleric,' Léon Dion has written. While the Church
stands at the centre of Canon Groulx's analysis of *la survivance,* Brunet is preoccupied with much more secular
problems, such as class structure, economic organization,
and political power. Nor is the lay historian unwilling to
criticize the Church, even cast doubt on its role of guaran-

teeing French-Canadian survival. All of this suggests, quite accurately, a very different outlook.

As a nationalist historian, Brunet starts from a novel position. Instead of glorifying the past as a 'golden age', he plays the role of debunker. His national past does not impress him. 'It is a past in which heroes and brilliant acts were very rare. A past in which men were only men. They are not less congenial for that. A past in which the *Canadiens*, our ancestors, our grandfathers, and our fathers, knew more defeats than victories. A past in which the failures have been more numerous than the successes. A past without greatness and without flourish to which we are the modest heirs.' As for the glorious struggles that guaranteed French Canada's survival, this self-styled enemy of 'wishful thinking' writes: 'This survival is not a collective success worthy of astonishment. It was the result of a combination of circumstances which the historian can easily analyse and which owe very little to the clear-sightedness of the *Canadiens* themselves.' These icy comments might well come from a writer profoundly hostile to French-Canadian nationalism. But to place Brunet in that category would be wholly misleading; his iconoclasm is the iconoclasm of the true nationalist believer. However, the demythologizing has only just begun.

Without a tear, Brunet condemns the whole corpus of traditional French-Canadian nationalist thought. 'Most of the theoreticians of French-Canadian nationalism were mistaken and have badly directed those who gave them their confidence,' he wrote in 1961. This sweeping condemnation is developed in one of Brunet's best and most controversial essays – one of the two essays that established him as an imaginative historian, the other being his account of the economic consequences of the Conquest. In his essay 'Trois dominantes de la pensée canadienne-française: l'agriculturisme, l'anti-étatisme, et le messian-isme', Brunet analyses and exposes the illusions that he believes have detrimentally dominated French-Canadian thought. Quite characteristically, he uses the bludgeon rather than the rapier. It was this essay that led André Laurendeau, who agreed with its general thesis, to write: 'Something tells me that these structures come a little too much from the historian's ideas and not enough from historical facts.' This remark could be applied to much of Brunet's writing; indeed, it is a characteristic of the nationalist school of history. Be that as it may, Brunet's analysis of the Arcadian ideal, the concept of the spiritual mission of French Canada in North America, and finally the fear of state intervention, is, in general terms, convincing. What, in effect, he is criticizing is the tendency of French-Canadian nationalist thinkers to withdraw from the real world of North American life, the life of an industrial and urban society.

Brunet demands that nationalists accept the facts of North American life and turn their backs on idle talk about the rural vocation and civilizing mission of French Canada. Instead, through the use of the state, a strong community capable of resisting assimilation could be built. Here he presents his view with passion: 'Vanquished and conquered, separated from their metropolitan power, deprived of a business class, poor and isolated, ignorant, reduced to a minority in the country that their ancestors had founded, colonized by an absentee capitalism, the French Canadians had an absolute need for the vigilant intervention of their provincial state.' Where most earlier nationalists viewed the church as the primary instrument of French-Canadian survival, the secular-minded Brunet is convinced that a modern nation requires an interventionist state to guarantee its existence.* Moreover, he recognizes that Confederation gave the French Canadians a provincial state with substantial powers. But, suffering from worn-out illusions and false spirituality, they failed to use it. The anti-clericalism implicit in this view of the state needs no emphasis.

But the question that arises is: why did the French Canadians suffer these illusions so long? The answer is in the central concept of Brunet's thought, the idea that lies at the basis of his whole armoury of sociological generalization, of historical *obiter dicta*, and, above all, of his nationalist doctrine. That concept is the Conquest. It is not that Brunet discovered the Conquest, though he sometimes speaks as though he had; but rather it is the way he interprets its effects that gives his view importance. Naturally the Conquest has always been seen as something of a tragedy for French Canadians, though the more clerical writers never failed to point out that it had saved French Canada from a worse fate – the French Revolution. For Brunet, that is merely a clerical illusion. In fact, the Conquest was the ultimate tragedy and for a startling reason, though not so startling when Brunet's secular assumptions are recalled. The Conquest, says the Montreal historian, brought the downfall of the French-Canadian middle class, leaving Quebec an 'abnormal society' suffering from 'social decapitation'. 'The absence of this directing and lay bourgeois class, whose role has been so important in the evolution of the societies of the Atlantic world, remains the great fact in the history of French Canada since the Conquest.'

*Here, as in many other places, Brunet is much less original in his views than appears on the surface. One writer, who like so many others was a victim of Brunet's criticism, expressed similar ideas on the necessity of state intervention fifty years before Brunet. (See Errol Bouchette, *L'Indépendance économique du Canada français*, third edition, Montreal, 1913.)

It is in his discussion of the consequences of the Conquest that Brunet the historian becomes Brunet the sociologist who has built a model of what a 'normal society' should be, measures his own society against the model, and finds it wanting. Since the middle class is, according to this model, the backbone of any normal society, it follows readily that French Canada was left nearly powerless when its bourgeoisie, cut off from its metropolitan sources of strength by the Conquest, was gradually replaced by an English middle class. The consequences of the Conquest, then, was a status of economic – and therefore political – inferiority among French Canadians.

Brunet's account of the fate of the French-Canadian middle class has not won unanimous agreement from his fellow historians. One school of economic historians doubts the very existence of any substantial middle class in New France, in the normally understood sense of that term. These writers argue that it was not the Conquest as much as the inefficiency and lack of a real bourgeois ethos that brought about the downfall of the French-Canadian merchants. Indeed, it appears that Brunet, with his profound concern about the present, began by correctly perceiving a contemporary problem that faces French Canada – the lack of a business class – and read it backwards into history to find its source in a traditional French-Canadian nationalist explanation: the Conquest. As so often with Brunet's intoxicating nationalist history, the bottle is new, but the wine fully aged.*

The Conquest was, of course, crucial to French Canada. It not only placed New France under a new metropolitan power, but also, through gradual immigration, transformed

*Some further discussion may be found in F.-A. Angers, 'Naissance de la pensée économique au Canada français', *Revue d'histoire de l'Amérique français*, Vol. XV, No. 2, September 1962, pages 204-29.

French Canadians into a minority. Here Brunet advances yet another of his influential hypotheses, perhaps his most influential one. The view is summed up in the title of his first collection of essays, *Canadians et Canadiens*. Briefly the thesis is that not one but two nations inhabit Canada, one Canadian or Anglo-Canadian, the other *canadien* or French-Canadian. Paraphrasing Durham, Brunet writes of 'two nationalisms opposing one another in the bosom of the same state'. Once again, then, in traditional nationalist fashion, Canadian history becomes a struggle of 'races' or nations. But as usual with Brunet, the old idea is given several new twists.

He rejects the old view that English Canadians are merely British colonials. He insists that English Canada is a nation, united by a powerful monolithic nationalism that is British in origin but Canadian in application and the interests it serves. Discussing Canadian involvement in Imperial wars, despite French-Canadian opposition, Brunet observes shrewdly: 'In all justice, it is necessary to say that if someone has sinned through nationalism in Canada, it is not the French Canadians.'

A second implication of the two-nations theory is much more important. Working from a concept (or rather an assumption) of power politics, Brunet argues that when two nations are associated within a single state the majority nation inevitably rules. But in order to have it both ways – that is, the majority rules in Canada but not in Quebec – he formulates his theory in this fashion: 'And, usually, minorities do not govern majorities. Except when the minority has economic control over the area in which it lives.' Thus the minority, the French Canadians, must become reconciled to the fact that in the last analysis the majority, the English Canadians, will rule.

It is a gloomy and pessimistic picture that emerges from

Brunet's description of the past and his assessment of the
French Canadians' present position. What can a French
Canadian do to better the position of his people, or at least
guarantee their survival? The answer is that he cannot do
very much. Primarily he must be realistic. He must never
expect that the minority can lead the majority. For Brunet,
there is no possibility that French Canadians might become
part of a majority through alliance with like-minded English Canadians because, by definition, there is no such
thing as a like-minded English Canadian. Race or nationality usually determines man's viewpoint; most certainly
in times of crisis. Of course Brunet cannot deny that French
and English politicians can and do work together, and that
this co-operation may be of some benefit to French Canadians. Essentially, however, he sees this co-operation (or,
in the more derogatory term that he prefers, collaboration)
as a means of disguising the naked power of the majority.
'In a state in which two nations coexist, the majority nation
must always take care to associate the minority nation with
its policy. It is thus less difficult to camouflage it as a common policy, though necessarily it remains no less the policy
of the majority nation.' Moreover, the leaders of French
Canada 'must never ask from the majority that which it
cannot give them. Their objectives ought to be modest but
feasible.'

There are two solutions to the problem of relations between Canadians and *Canadiens*. Brunet dismisses these
with particular disdain. The first is separatism. In 1954
he wrote that English Canada would never tolerate separatism, and that it possessed the political, economic, and
military means to enforce its will. Quebec separatists, he
remarked, 'would have an interest in studying the history
of the Confederacy'. Equally chimerical for those who wish
to preserve French Canada is the belief that Canada can

become a bilingual and bicultural nation. 'For some years, the prophets of a new order have been inviting the French Canadians of Quebec to make Canada a bi-ethnic and bicultural country. Those who propose such a program forget – by simple ignorance, because they have the bad habit of mistaking their desires for reality, or with the intention of betraying the good faith of the minority – that Canada is an English country inside of which a French-Canadian province survives as a veritable economic and political colony of the Anglo-Canadian nation.' Indeed, those who advocate this utopian policy of biculturalism and bilingualism have really ceased to be French Canadians. Above all, perhaps, French Canadians must be on their guard against politicians who prate about national unity; for, given the inevitable predominance of the majority, national unity can only mean the suppression of the minority. It is a slogan used by the majority to obtain from the minority something that it would not dare ask for in its own name.

Since national unity is a trap for French Canadians, those who advocate it are in effect the enemies of French Canada. And since it is not only English Canadians but also some French Canadians who favour national unity, Brunet calls forth and subtly broadens the old concept of the *vendu*. Nearly the whole historical leadership of French Canada is condemned for collaboration with the Conqueror and the preservation of the Conqueror's myths. For example, he damns those French Canadians who have dared to suggest that the Conquest may have brought some benefits to French Canadians. 'The *Canadiens* are told', he wrote in 1959, 'that, thanks to the cleverness of their religious and political leaders and their own courage, they have finally successfully overcome all the bad consequences of a foreign domination. The French-Canadian ruling classes – whose accession to a position of pre-eminence has always depended on the willingness of either the British authorities or the English-Canadian leaders – are interested in upholding this historical interpretation.' In short, the traditional leaders of French Canada were Quislings. But the *vendu* category is broadened even further to include those French-Canadian intellectuals, especially the 'social leftists', who find French-Canadian nationalism somewhat stifling and hence reject it or at least seriously criticize it. Finally, there are 'the businessmen, engineers, politicians who make their living with British Canada or need to make friends among English-speaking people. One can easily understand why they speak and act as they do.' The fact of the matter seems to be that all those French Canadians, past and present, who have failed to accept Brunet's particular brand of nationalism have at best been stupid wishful thinkers, at worst traitors. This type of argument is a familiar one, but the familiarity only makes its logical inadequacies more obvious.

If all these activities are suspect, is anything left for French Canadians who 'have long since lost, as a nation, their right to self-determination'? According to Brunet, there is only one possible salvation: vigilant defence of provincial autonomy. Once more the radical turns into the traditionalist, for no political strategy is more marked by the persistent usage of the past than autonomism. But for Brunet, Quebec is the nation-state of French Canada; the diaspora is to be forgotten, doomed to assimilation. Ottawa must be recognized and accepted as the national capital of English Canada, Quebec of French Canada.

For the French Canadians, the government at Ottawa can only be the central government of a federation uniting Quebec and English Canada. A close and harmonious collaboration can and should exist between the federal and the provincial authorities. However, the government charged with defending and promoting the common good of the French-Canadian nationality is the one of the province where the immense majority of the French Canadians live. That is why Quebec ought not to be considered or to consider itself simply as one of ten provinces. It has the right to claim a special status in the Canadian federation since it is the spokesman and defender of the minority.

But provincial autonomy must be more than mere intransigent defence of the constitutional rights of the province. The powers of the province must be used and the old anti-statist illusions rejected. Even the report of the Tremblay Commission, with its voluminous examination and defence of provincial autonomy, Brunet dismisses as 'the summation of traditional nationalism with all its illusions and all its contradictions'. Moreover, he found little to praise in the Union Nationale régime: 'imitating the federal Liberals of the Lapointe-Cardin period, it knew how to exploit with ease the feeling of insecurity, the traditional ideals and the collectivity's instinct for solidarity.' Still, the Union Nationale did defend provincial autonomy and therefore was never severely criticized by Brunet. But the main point is that the time had come for French Canadians to allow their provincial state to play the role they had denied it since the Conquest. A new policy of state intervention, a new 'socialisme royal' such as that practised under the Old Régime by Jean Talon, was necessary if French Canadians were to survive as a twentieth-century industrial and urban society.

Brunet's belief that a form of survival could be ensured through positive autonomy is the one ray of optimism in an otherwise dark picture. His views, and those of the school for which he is the most articulate spokesman, have been given the title of 'pessimistic nationalism'. In some nationalist circles, particularly those still dominated by Canon Groulx's more optimistic and clerical teachings, *brunetisme* won as many enemies as friends. Here is one comment that reveals a good deal about the function of education in a nationalist community: 'In struggling against a style, M. Brunet ends by removing from us the reasons for living and struggling. His irresponsible exaggerations cause incalculable harm to certain young people, and risk killing, by excessive and badly advised criticism, all patriotic education.'

But such criticism, fair as it was, failed to foresee that Brunet's views by their very pessimism could stimulate a reaction more potent than romantic optimism could ever hope to achieve. The criticisms missed the fundamental point that, above all, Brunet too was a nationalist. The historian himself described the function of his iconoclastic analysis: 'National history, gilt-edged and falsified by patriotic emotion, has no educational value. Students, when they have passed the age in which they believed in fairy tales, take a dislike to the study of a history that has no connection with reality and with the present. On becoming adults, the new generations notice that the lives that they are called to live do not correspond to the pastoral idyll that preceding generations have lived. They search in vain to explain to themselves this solution to the continuity between the idealized past and the severely realistic present.' In the new realistic perspective, the past is brought into accurate focus with all its failures and weaknesses. Then it becomes clear that the present can only be reformed by rejecting the old illusions. The world of industrialization and urbanization must be accepted and rural myths forgotten; the spiritual messianism of the past must be replaced by the material needs of the present; the fear of the state must be eradicated, and this instrument of survival allowed to undertake the tasks that all modern societies give it. Thus the old nationalism is denounced to give place to the new.

While these implications of Brunet's history are obvious, there are others that are no less so. Though Brunet himself rejects separatism, his 'national doctrine' could easily, even logically, lead to it. First there is the postulation of two distinct, even opposing, nations. Then there is the theory that the lion necessarily takes the lion's share. What could be more reasonable than to conclude that the only way French Canada can guarantee its survival and live a 'normal' life is to end the political association in which the smaller nation is really nothing more than a 'colony' annexed to the larger nation? In short, the implication of pessimistic nationalism is that, given the Conquest, French Canada is doomed. And if the Conquest lies at the root of the society's problems, and the existing constitutional machinery of Canada rests on that Conquest, then Confederation must de undone and with it the Conquest. In short, whatever other conclusions are possible, there can be no question that separatism is one conclusion that may be drawn from the teachings of the school of Brunet. To the logical young mind, dissatisfied with a status quo so obviously unsatisfactory when judged by the Brunet criteria, separation is obviously preferable to the third clearly implied alternative: assimilation. It is not surprising that the two-nations theory underlies the separatist argument, for separatism is, after all, merely another attempt to undo the decision of 1759.*

Obviously the foundation of Brunet's view is found in Durham's 'two nations warring in the bosom of a single

*See, for example, two books by Raymond Barbeau, *J'ai choisi l'indé-pendance* (Montreal, 1961), and *Québec, est-il une colonie?* (Montreal, 1962).

state'. The fact that Durham vastly overstated and over-simplified the events that led up to 1837 does not shake Brunet's faith in the theory. It would take a book to disprove the application of the theory, but at least a few questions can be raised now. If 1837 was a 'racial conflict', how, first of all, can its narrow base be explained; and secondly, how are similar events in 'racially' homogeneous Upper Canada explained? Another example that Brunet chooses as an illustration of his Canadian-*Canadien* dichotomy is the debate over the Canadian contribution to the Boer War. In this debate, he says, Laurier represented the Canadian viewpoint calling for participation, Bourassa the *canadien* viewpoint calling for abstention. If only history were that simple. In fact, Laurier's moderation on the South African question infuriated many English Canadians, as the 1900 election returns showed. As for Bourassa, it is true that his anti-Imperial sentiments found much sympathy in Quebec. It is also true, however, that the Quebec electorate showed no doubts whatever about Laurier in 1900. And, finally, a detail worth noting is that Bourassa himself based his hostility to participation in the Boer War on what he considered a Canadian attitude toward Imperial responsibilities, an attitude defined in the first instance by Sir John A. Macdonald. In nearly every instance, with the possible exception of the conscription crises of 1917 and 1942 (and even these need qualification), the Brunet thesis fails to explain all the facts. In the past, French and English Canadians, beginning with Lafontaine and Baldwin, have in practice rejected Durham's dichotomy.

But Durham's views, which infuriate most French Canadians, exercise a peculiar magnetism on Brunet, who once called the English lord 'the best historian of Canada'. Brunet seems torn between two alternatives: on the one hand is the suspicion that Durham was accurate in his analysis of the causes of the 1837 affair and therefore right in his prescription of assimilation; on the other his nationalist commitment to *la survivance*. Brunet the social scientist attempts to use Durham's analysis without reaching the conclusions that are repugnant to Brunet the nationalist. But the fact that the tension between assimilation and survival remains unresolved in Brunet's own mind explains why his followers, unable to live with the unresolved tension, are forced to choose one of the alternatives – frequently separatism, frequently one of its variants. Had Brunet accepted Durham's analysis and solution, his apparent radicalism would be more convincing. Among many contemporary nationalists, there is a natural demand that radical analysis should produce radical conclusions.*

Conclusions more moderate in tone than separatism can also be drawn from Brunet's 'national doctrine'. One such conclusion – though it is really only a separatist variant – has been drawn by the Montreal branch of the Société Saint-Jean-Baptiste, of which Brunet is an officer. The society's submission to the Quebec Legislature's Committee on the Constitution is the distilled essence of *brunetisme*. It rings all the changes on Canadian and *Canadien*, majorities and minorities, conquerors and conquered. 'Will the French Canadians', the submission asks, 'form the last colonized people on earth?'

To this question the old pessimistic Brunet, with his harsh deterministic theory of majorities and minorities, would surely have answered in the affirmative. But a change

*For an article by a writer to whom Brunet attributes many of his ideas and who makes the separatist implications of pessimistic nationalism clear, see Maurice Séguin, 'Genèse et historique de l'idée séparatiste au Canada français', *Laurentie*, No. 119, June 1962, pages 940-96.

has taken place in Quebec. A new nationalism, which certainly owes something to the teachings of the Montreal historian, has flowered. Reform has begun, a reform that quite frankly rejects at least the illusions of ruralism and anti-statism, if not messianism. In short, the minority nation is proving that it can do something. Indeed, only the most blindly deterministic two-nations theorist would deny that the so-called minority nation is having a marked impact on the majority nation. These changes have not failed to influence the views of even a social scientist as convinced of his Olympian detachment as Michel Brunet. A note of optimism has appeared that is new, although it grows directly out of his appeal for 'positive autonomism'. The submission of the Société Saint-Jean-Baptiste states: 'Endowed with a self-confidence which they have up to now lacked, French Canadians of 1964, rejecting the fatalistic option of their fathers, seem decided to orient their history by themselves and for themselves.'

The conclusion that the Société Saint-Jean-Baptiste of Montreal drew from its survey of Canadian history, guided by the principles of *brunetisme*, was that Canada needed an entirely new constitution. Two nations require two states that will be associated with one another in a federal structure in which each nation will be equally represented. This submission and its conclusions indicate the extent to which Brunet's theories have become orthodox nationalist assumptions, even in an organization as traditionalist as the Société Saint-Jean-Baptiste.

The widespread influence of *brunetisme* – that combination of iconoclasm and conservatism (or as Laurier said of Bourassa, that *Castor-rouge* mixture that is French-Canadian nationalism) – provides a key to an understanding of contemporary Quebec. And that key is found in the nature and limits of Brunet's debunking attitude towards the past. An insecure society rarely produces debunkers, for it fears most the enemy within. The historical fashions of the United States in the fifties, which down-graded debunking, provide an example. But a society in the process of profound changes, changes that defy the conventional wisdom, seems to produce vigorous criticism of the past. The United States in the thirties is an obvious example.

Brunet's writings coincide with a period of great change in French Canada, a period during which nearly all traditional values are being questioned. Yet Brunet's commitment to debunking is very limited, for he never questions the system of nationalism but only its traditional justification. He is, then, a conservative debunker. An example of radical criticism, a writer who questions the system itself, is Pierre-Elliott Trudeau. This explains an important division in contemporary Quebec. As long as traditionalist nationalism in the form of Maurice Duplessis's Union Nationale held power, all the critics stood together in opposition. But once the Duplessis régime was replaced by a reform administration, the former allies-in-opposition discovered that their ultimate objectives had always been different. For men like Trudeau, nationalism itself lies at the root of French Canada's problems. Therefore they find the new nationalism as deficient in principle, if not in practice, as the old. The other school, which might be called the René Lévesque school, really follows Brunet in rejecting only the traditionalist aspects of nationalism. For them, nationalism is valid if brought into conformity with the social and economic needs of modern society. The Lévesque-cum-Brunet school is currently the predominant one in Quebec, but the Trudeau anti-nationalist (or, more correctly, Actonian multi-nationalist) view is far from having been proven invalid.

The explanation for the popularity of Brunet's austere

'national doctrine' is not far to seek. Despite Brunet's apparent radical iconoclasm, his basic approach to the history of his people is orthodox. History for him, as for previous nationalist historians, is a weapon to be wielded in the unceasing national struggle. Though Brunet is a professional historian, most of his published works are 'sermons for the unsatisfied'. His own research is largely limited to the period immediately following the Conquest, and even here his conclusions have been challenged. As he moves into less familiar areas, his ability to generalize dogmatically grows apace. Indeed, there is even reason to suspect that Professor Brunet aspires to write 'metahistory' in company with Arnold Toynbee, whom the French-Canadian historian has vigorously criticized. But is not Brunet himself something of the 'prestidigitateur' for whom history is a bag of nationalist tricks? Like Toynbee, he is better at diagnosing the ills of society than at prescribing remedies, a fact that may raise doubts about both his diagnosis and the remedies proposed by his followers. 'The time has come for history, in French Canada, to give up the chair of rhetoric, according to the expression of Professor Trudel.' One wonders if this sound advice can be accepted as long as nationalist objectives dominate the historian's approach.

EIGHT

The Canadian Dilemma: Locke, Rousseau, or Acton?

'There are two miracles in Canadian history,' Professor F. R. Scott of McGill University once maintained. 'The first is the survival of French Canada, and the second is the survival of Canada.' Almost always in the past English Canadians and more particularly French Canadians have believed instinctively that these two miracles were linked indissolubly together. Most French Canadians were convinced that *la survivance de la nation canadienne-française* depended on an alliance with English Canada, and even on the protection of the British Empire. The theme that the 'last cannon-shot which booms on this continent in defence of Great Britain' will be 'fired by the hands of a French Canadian' is an important one in the history of French Canada.

Then, too, one of the most frequently repeated arguments in favour of the acceptance of Confederation in 1865 was that it was the only alternative to annexation. That argument has often been adapted for modern usage. Pointing out the weakness of the French-Canadian separatist case a few years ago, M. André Laurendeau wrote: 'Above all, one of the principal motives which led to the creation of Canada: the proximity of a large country to the south and the necessity of gathering together the British colonies in order to allow them to exist beside the United States, this motive has become more imperious. A segmented Canada would have scarcely more influence than one of the little republics of central America: would it even be able to exist?' From the French-Canadian viewpoint it has always been obvious that although they were a minority in Canada, they would be an even smaller and more precarious group, and therefore less capable of resisting absorption into the United States, if they attempted to exist apart from English Canada.

The irony of today's situation is that while a growing number of English Canadians have concluded that the survival of Canada can best be guaranteed by continuing the French-English association, there are now a growing number of French Canadians who are no longer convinced that the miracle of *la survivance* depends on this alliance. This latter is not yet a predominant view, but it is threatening enough to cause James Eayrs to remark recently: 'This crisis of nationhood presents to a Prime Minister of Canada an issue transcending all others in urgency and importance. For many years it was his main concern so to conduct his countrymen's affairs that there would continue to be two sovereign governments in North America, not one. Today his main concern is that there continue to be two sovereign governments not three.'

Canada's present 'crisis of nationhood' is at least partly explained by the old symbol of 'two solitudes'. For reasons attributable largely, though certainly not exclusively, to the majority, French and English Canadians have rarely understood one another's purposes. That is the central failure of the Canadian experiment and one for which we are bound to continue paying heavily until it is rectified. In Canada we have only rarely conformed to Durham's famous description of 'two nations warring in the bosom of a single state'. But, what may be worse, we have been two nations each talking to itself within the bosom of a single state.

Perhaps the most extraordinary thing about Canada is that while French and English Canadians have interacted upon each other to an immeasurable extent, the two people hardly know one another. What is today fashionably called a 'national style' is, in Canada, almost wholly a reflection of the delicately balanced relationship between French- and English-speaking Canadians. Few if any other countries exemplify the obsession with that holy grail of all Canadian politicians, 'national unity'. That is only one example of what has been called the 'bifocal' character of Canada. Nor should it be necessary to insist that the character of French-Canadian nationalism can only be understood when it is placed in the matrix of French-English relations in Canada. But despite the obvious impact of each group on the other, there is only a very limited interchange between the two groups. English Canadians read American and British newspapers, magazines, and novels, and of course watch American movies and television programs. Most of them could not, even if they wanted to, read a French-Canadian novel or understand a French-language television commentator. It is almost certainly true that an undergraduate in an English-Canadian university spends more time reading about the history of Great Britain and the United States than he does reading about the history of French Canada. Whatever else a young French-Canadian undergraduate in history may learn, he spends very little time on the history of English Canada except where it relates to *la survivance*. Mr. George Ferguson, a shrewd observer of the Canadian scene, once observed that 'because of differences of race and language, culture and tradition, and, to some extent, religion, Quebec remains a *terra incognita* to almost all English Canadians.' And English Canada is almost as much of a mystery to French Canadians.

While language is obviously an important wall between French and English Canadians, history, perhaps, divides us even more. The central event in the history of Canada is the British Conquest in 1760. Whatever this event may have meant in the lives of eighteenth-century French Canadians (and there is a good deal of scholarly dispute on that subject) it is nevertheless true that since the beginning of the nineteenth century French-Canadian nationalists have been attempting to overcome it. And the French-Canadian nationalist quite naturally identifies the Conqueror of 1760 with his rather indirect heir, the contemporary English Canadian. Actually, though one occasionally hears crude remarks about the Plains of Abraham, English Canadians are largely unconscious of their Conqueror's role. But consciously or not the Conquest dominates English-Canadian nationalism, just as it does French-Canadian nationalism, giving the former a sense of belonging to the winning side, the latter a yearning for lost glories. The Conquest, then, is the burden of Canadian history.

It is at least partly the Conquest that explains the different public philosophies of French and English Canada. Because they are a conquered people and a minority, French Canadians have always been chiefly concerned with group rights. Their public philosophy might be called Rousseauian: the expression of a 'general will' to survive. The English Canadian, as is equally befitting his majority position, is far more concerned with individual rights and with that characteristic North American middle-class ideal, equality of opportunity. The English Canadian's public philosophy might be somewhat grandly described as Lockean. The English Canadian has therefore tended to look upon privileges asked for or granted to groups as inherently undesirable, indeed undemocratic. This means, then, especially since the dominant English-Canadian tradition is Protestant, that rights granted to groups *as* French Canadians or *as* Roman Catholics are at best an unfortunate deviation from the democratic norm, at worst a devilish plot to undermine Canadian, that is English-Canadian Protestant, civilization. The English Canadian instinctively makes the natural but nevertheless arrogant majoritarian assumption that the only fair and just way to run a society is according to the well-known Australian principle of 'one bloody man, one bloody vote'. The French Canadian just as instinctively makes the no less natural, and not always less arrogant, minoritarian assumption that a truly fair and just society would be based on something closer to the principle of representation by groups. And most French Canadians insist that there are only two groups in Canada.

It is this basic difference in public philosophy that divides Canadians. To an extent, I think to a quite successful extent, our political and constitutional machinery was designed to overcome or at least blur this difference. The federal system has meant, or at least was intended to mean, that those things most fundamental to the survival of the minority culture are placed safely beyond the reach of the majority. By defending provincial autonomy French Canadians could, in the past, defend at least a large part of the French-Canadian nation. At the same time our federal parties have usually worked in such a way as to ensure that if vigorous leaders were sent to Ottawa by Quebec something very near to a French-Canadian veto could be exercised within the federal cabinet, at least in matters that touched on French-Canadian affairs. It is true that the veto has not always been effective, though history unfortunately records more clearly those cases where it failed — Riel,

conscription, and so on. History says less about the cases
where the veto succeeded. When the complete story of Canadian foreign policy in the inter-war years is revealed,
the influence of a man like Ernest Lapointe will almost
certainly appear enormous. But the main point is, and it
has often been made, that the Baldwin–Lafontaine, Macdonald–Cartier, Laurier–Sifton, King–Lapointe, St. Laurent–Howe tradition has given French Canadians a role
in federal politics somewhat greater than a strict adherence to the principle of representation by population
would have provided. Within the federal cabinet, the leading French Canadian is not a minister like the others.

But while our federal constitution allows Quebec a large
measure of autonomy and our federal parties are especially
susceptible to French-Canadian influence, one part of the
French-Canadian community is left unprotected in practice if not in theory. These are the French Canadians living
beyond the frontiers of the mother province. And it is here
that English Canada's Lockean approach takes its toll.
While Quebec is a constitutionally bilingual province, the
other provinces, except for a brief two decades in Manitoba, have been unilingual. English-speaking Protestant
majorities in every province, as far as the constitution per-
mitted, have reduced the privileges of Roman Catholic and
French-speaking minorities to a minimum. Whether the
reason has been religious or national is difficult to decide
with certainty, though it was probably religious in Manitoba in 1890 and national in Ontario in 1912. While the
constitution in some cases (Ontario for example) has protected religious separate schools in a limited way, it gives
no protection to French-language rights. The Fathers of
Confederation had not seen fit to provide such guarantees;
so where French-language schools existed by custom they
have been eliminated by measures that are, according to

the courts, within the letter of the constitution. Whether these measures are also within the spirit of the constitution is a matter that neither courts nor historians can decide with certainty. The effect of these actions has been to make French Canadians outside Quebec a minority like any other, subject, in matters of education, to the same laws as others.

Nowhere has this point been better established than in the case of Manitoba. Under the Laurier–Greenway settlement of 1897, which was designed to restore some of the privileges that the Roman Catholic and French-speaking minorities had been deprived of by the Manitoba School Act of 1890, bilingual schools meant English and *any* other language demanded by a minority group. And in 1916, when these bilingual schools were abolished, the public-school system's *Kulturkampf* was directed not only against German, Ukrainian, and Icelandic immigrants, but also against Franco-Manitobans. The survival of the French-speaking minorities outside Quebec, and they have survived in varying degrees, is a minor miracle attributable only to the will of these people to live according to the dictates of their culture. It is only recently, and very belatedly, that a growing number of English Canadians have recognized that the survival of the French-speaking minority groups is one important guarantee of Quebec's continued interest in Confederation.

Not unnaturally, French Canadians have developed a profound sense of grievance about the manner in which their compatriots were treated in the other provinces. This sense of grievance has been deepened enormously, of course, by the presence in Quebec of an English-speaking minority enjoying complete equality of rights in the educational system and bilingualism in public affairs, and to a large extent dominating the economy of the province.

Despite repeated rebuffs in their attempts to extend French-language rights outside Quebec, most French-Canadian nationalists before 1945 refused to abandon the hope that one day the minorities in the other provinces would receive more equitable treatment. In 1913 Henri Bourassa stated the basic argument for this view when he said: 'The Canadian Confederation . . . is the result of a contract between the two races, French and English, treating on an equal footing and recognizing equal rights and reciprocal obligations. The Canadian Confederation will last only to the extent that the equality of rights will be recognized as the basis of public law in Canada, from Halifax to Vancouver.' As long as the French-Canadian nationalist believed that a bicultural Canada was possible, then he refused to identify the nation with the province.

Since 1945, and especially during the last decade, there has been a growing tendency for French-Canadian nationalists to write off the minorities, maintaining that the unending ransom being paid for these hostages to Confederation is a poor investment. As René Lévesque commented, referring to the Royal Commission on Bilingualism and Biculturalism: 'It is infinitely more important to make Quebec progressive, free, and strong than to devote the best of our energies to propagating the doubtful advantages of biculturalism.' The assumption underlying this view is, of course, that the province is identified with the nation. This explains the significance of the 'recent but now common usage, *l'Etat du Québec*.

But this 'nationalization' of the province is not merely the result of disillusionment about the fate of the minorities. It is also a response to a series of developments in English Canada. In the years immediately following the Second World War, English Canadians became increasingly self-conscious, even nationalistic. For one thing, they had played an important role in defeating the Axis powers. And largely because of the political skill of Mackenzie King and the political realism of Louis St. Laurent, the country that emerged from the war's two conscription crises had only a few scars on its unity.

Then, too, after 1945 Canadians suddenly realized that the traditional balance of power in their North American world had been badly upset. Where Britain had once stood as a material and psychological counter-balance against Canada's closest neighbour, the war had exhausted Britain and catapulted the United States into a position of world pre-eminence. This is what Professor F. H. Underhill has called 'the revolution of 1940' when 'we passed from the British century of our history to the American century. . . . And', he added, 'our American century is going to be a much tougher experience for us than our British century was.' Faced with this new situation, many Canadians concluded that public policies, national policies, would have to be devised to bolster up Canada's lonely independence. For English Canadians this meant action by Ottawa in economic, social, and cultural affairs on an unprecedented scale. And if these fears of the American giant were not enough to impel our politicians in the direction of the interventionist state, then the wartime industrialization and urbanization provided the necessary additional impetus.

Most English Canadians, the majority of whom voted for a federal party led by a French Canadian, were unpleasantly surprised to find that Quebec was hesitant about accepting the new nationalist role that the federal government was assuming. After all, we were all Canadians (though evidently some were more Canadian than others). Ottawa belonged to all of us. Why should the federal government not, therefore, move into these new fields even if it did encroach on such traditionally provincial responsibilities as education and social welfare? The difficulty with this point of view was that many French Canadians feared that the new 'Canadianism', promoted by Ottawa, ignored or perhaps even threatened '*Canadienisme*'. As the Ligue d'Action Nationale remarked in its submission to the Royal Commission on the Arts, Letters and Sciences in 1950: 'Current language frequently makes use of the expressions "Canadian nation", "Canadian culture". This manner of speaking is not in itself reprehensible provided that no one draws from there a complete theory of Canadian national unity.'

But few English Canadians paid any attention to this view, for in their eyes provincial autonomy and French-Canadian nationalism had been largely discredited. After all, Premier Duplessis was not only a nationalist and an autonomist but also remarkably illiberal and corrupt. Most English Canadians concluded, therefore, that French-Canadian nationalism was merely a tool used by a reactionary provincial politician to undermine the progressive policies of Ottawa. Thus, happily, the new Canadian nationalism seemed to coincide with progressivism and modernism. French-Canadian nationalism was just as obviously backward and obsolete. M. Duplessis and his Union Nationale abundantly proved everything that most English Canadians had long, secretly or openly, believed about French-Canadian nationalism. And they were often encouraged in this view by the foes of *duplessisme* in Quebec.

Thus there developed the opinion in English Canada that if Quebec was ever to come to terms with the chrome-plated, modern world of North America it would first have to shed its parochial nationalism. As late as three years after the death of Premier Duplessis, and two years after M. Lesage's reforming Liberals had entered office, the Toronto *Globe and Mail* expressed exactly this view in explaining its opposition to the appointment of a royal commission on bilingualism and biculturalism:'A wiser course, in our view,' the editor noted, 'would be to let Quebec complete the task it has set itself. The Province is now in good hands, and the necessary basic reforms have been initiated. If we have patience, the discovery already made by its leaders, that English is the language of commerce and is as essential to Quebec as to the rest of us, will spread throughout the populace. We will find wider areas of agreement. French-speaking Canadians will retain their culture, as the Welsh and Scotch have done. We will be able in time to find the unity we seek.'

That comment is enormously revealing. First, one may note, it was the type of attitude that was driving many young French Canadians into the nationalist and separatist catacombs. M. André Laurendeau, the editor-in-chief of *Le Devoir*, wrote in commenting on the *Globe*'s condescending observations: 'Were the *Globe and Mail* editorial a true reflection of English Canada today, I, with many others, would become a separatist. I would go to this extremity without joy; and would, in self-defence, curse those who had forced me to it. But a fundamental instinct and desire to live despite it all would nevertheless keep me going.' M. Laurendeau is now, as the co-chairman of the Royal Commission the *Globe* unsuccessfully opposed, engaged full-time in attempting to discover how far the Toronto paper's views were the views of English Canada. It should be added that in the last year or so the attitude of the *Globe and Mail* towards Quebec has been enormously liberalized.

M. Laurendeau was probably right in thinking that in 1962 the *Globe*'s opinions were not those of all English Canada. Two years earlier the case might have been different. Most English Canadians welcomed the defeat of the crumbling, corrupt Union Nationale government in June 1960. The victory of the Liberals led by the familiar former federal minister, Jean Lesage, seemed to promise the end of corruption, authoritarianism, and even that parochial spirit that French Canadians insisted on calling 'nationalism'. For most English Canadians autonomism and *duplessisme* were inseparable. It was for this reason that they had almost completely ignored the report of the Tremblay Commission in 1956. This commission, established by Premier Duplessis to examine the constitution, provided the most complete statement of autonomism ever devised. Had English Canadians read it they might have been better prepared for the events of the last two or three years. But since it was a product of the Union Nationale régime it was largely ignored.

With the Union Nationale gone, it was widely assumed that autonomism would soon disappear too. The new Quebec premier was given an exceedingly good press in English Canada during his first two years in office. He was often paid that highest English-Canadian compliment of having his name suggested as the successor to Lester Pearson. This suggestion may, of course, have been as much a reflection on Mr. Pearson as it was on M. Lesage. Anyway, M. Lesage was seen as the new Laurier who would bind up the nation's wounds as they were beginning to appear at the end of the Diefenbaker era. And among M. Lesage's ministers few were more popular during those early years than M. René Lévesque, who seemed, at least to liberal intellectuals always in search of an idol, to be the epitome of the intellectual *engagé*.

Of course there were still troubles between Ottawa and Quebec. But it was well known that all Quebec politicians, even Liberal ones, had to pay lip-service to provincial autonomy. And, moreover, there was the fact that Liberal provincial governments were almost duty-bound to fight with Conservative federal administrations – and vice versa. On towards the second year of the Lesage régime a growing number of people were happy to see the Quebec government adding its weight to the anti-Diefenbaker forces. This would surely aid in the return to office of the federal Liberals who, as everyone knew, have always been the trusted guardians of that highest Canadian virtue, 'national unity'. Indeed, there were many who still believed – or were convinced by Mr. Diefenbaker – that the late Mackenzie King, following a recipe secretly passed on to him by Sir Wilfrid Laurier, had actually invented 'national unity'. Once the country was returned to that almost divinely ordained condition of 'rouge à Ottawa et rouge à Québec', all would be for the best again.

Yet even before that blissful condition was achieved in the spring of 1963, there was a growing amount of evidence to suggest that the Lesage Liberals were not entirely orthodox. First there was the decision to place the privately-owned power companies under Hydro-Québec. While public ownership of electricity is hardly an unorthodox policy in Canada, the Quebec move was preceded by an election in which the Liberals campaigned on the nationalist slogan 'maîtres chez nous'. The nationalization was carried off in such a businesslike fashion, especially when compared with the much more arbitrary actions a year earlier of that Lochinvar of the West, Premier W. A. C. Bennett, that whatever fears had been raised were quickly laid. If English Canadians had known much about the educational history of Quebec they would have had another warning of the untraditional character of the Lesage Liberals when the decision to establish a ministry of education was announced. Here, in cold fact, was the civil authority imposing its will in an area traditionally held sacrosanct by the Church. But to most English Canadians a minister of education was the most natural thing in the world. Indeed, it was just another sign that French Canadians were at last recognizing the value of English-Canadian practices. Many English Canadians, of course, also approved of actions designed at last to put the Church in its place. It is worth adding that while for Quebec the Lesage reforms represent sizeable changes, most of them are fairly orthodox in the English-Canadian provinces. That is one reason why English Canadians did not get overly excited about the early events of 'la révolution tranquille'.

As the quiet revolution grew noisier and more expensive, English Canadians began to grow disturbed and to some extent hostile. The Quebec noise stretched all the way from the much-publicized separatist groups to the increasing number of statements by Premier Lesage and his ministers that the constitution, at least as it was being operated, was too restrictive of the ambitions of the 'Etat du Québec'. M. René Lévesque, known to be the *éminence grise* behind the power nationalization, was increasingly viewed with suspicion as he dropped off-the-cuff remarks that showed a shocking lack of respect for national unity. Indeed, by 1962 Quebec was more of an enigma to most English Canadians than it had ever been under M. Duplessis. In those good old days Quebec had seemed to have only one face and one voice. Moreover, since M. Duplessis had been a sound conservative, his autonomism had not cost the federal government much money. In both these respects the new régime in Quebec was quite different.

In the first place the autonomism of the Lesage government was guided by a program of positive nationalism. This included large expenditures for economic development, educational expansion, and social welfare programs. These were to be provincial policies designed and paid for by the provincial government. But to pay for these policies M. Lesage had to begin a campaign to push the federal government at least part way out of the fields of direct taxation that under the British North America Act are shared by the federal and provincial governments. This new conflict in federal-provincial relations might best be explained by noting that under M. Duplessis the provincial state was largely non-interventionist and passive; under M. Lesage the role of the state is positive and thus comes into direct competition with another interventionist state, Ottawa. By April 1963, when M. Lesage issued his famous 'ultimatum' or 'request' (depending on your translator) that Quebec should have 25 per cent of income taxes, 25 per cent of corporation taxes, and 100 per cent of succession taxes, English Canadians had come to realize that living with the new Quebec would cost money.

But the second upsetting fact about the new Quebec was that it no longer had one face and one voice. Indeed there were times when it appeared that even the government had several voices, of which the soothing tones of Jean Lesage and the rasping wit of René Lévesque were but two. And in addition to this multi-voiced government, after the 1962 general election, there appeared an even more confusing phenomenon in the person of M. Réal Caouette and some two dozen Social Credit M.P.s. If to some English Canadians René Lévesque was becoming a beardless Castro, M. Caouette was more reminiscent of an earlier generation of authoritarian radicals. And, if this was not enough, there was soon also an unharmonious chorus composed of nearly every French-Canadian newspaper, periodical, academic, radio and television commentator, student organization, and what not, advancing criticisms of Quebec's place in Confederation. And more often than not these criticisms were more precise than were the proffered alternatives –

except of course in the case of separatism. While it annoyed French Canadians to hear it said, it is really no wonder that, faced with this babel of raucous voices, English
Canadians began to demand somewhat impatiently, 'What
does Quebec want?'

And here we arrive at the nub of the problem. English
Canadians had grown used to hearing one voice from Quebec – whether it was Laurier or Duplessis. M. Duplessis
had often made clear what he wanted; English Canadians
had more often than not rejected his demands. Now, since
1960, there is no longer one voice. (Of course, there never
really was only one voice, but M. Duplessis succeeded in
making it seem so.) What distresses English Canadians is
their inability to get a single, clear statement of what Quebec would like to have done to make Confederation more
habitable. And this makes them suspect that either there is
no real grievance or the list of demands knows no end.
Many English Canadians, however, believe that enough of
what they call 'concessions' have already been made to
Quebec – perhaps too many. First there was the establishment of the Royal Commission on Bilingualism and Biculturalism; next the obvious steps to increase bilingualism in
the federal civil service; then the gradual decentralization
in order to allow more tax resources to the provinces and
more freedom to the provinces in policy choices. Then came
the crowning touch – the flag! Much of the debate has
centred on the flag because it is the kind of issue that ordi-
nary minds, like that of the leader of the Progressive Conservative Party, can understand. But the heat of that debate
is at least partly attributable to a vague feeling of unease
about Quebec's 'demands'. In fact the somewhat hostile
response to the so-called 'concessions' to Quebec is explained by the instinctive English-Canadian suspicion of

special treatment. Once more Locke and Rousseau have come into conflict.

English Canadians are right in believing that French Canadians are asking to be treated as though they were not the same as other Canadians, and as though Quebec 'n'est pas une province comme les autres'. What French Canadians are asking for is equality. There are, of course, many different prescriptions being offered for the achievement of that equality. English Canada's response to the demand for equality depends on how far the prescription requires them to give up their traditional Lockean assumptions. The more nationalist the prescription, that is to say, the closer the French Canadian comes to saying that our present system based on a modified version of 'rep by pop' must be replaced by a system of representation by nations, the less sympathetic English Canadians are likely to be.

Recently, a young journalist who over the past three years has done much to try to inform English Canadians of events in Quebec published 'An Open Letter to the French-Canadian Nationalists', which probably sums up a good deal of the thinking among English Canadians who have been somewhat sympathetic to the aspirations of Quebec. These people have been upset by the increasing intensity of the nationalism of Quebec, and the apparent unwillingness of Quebeckers to pay any attention to the people of good will in English Canada. 'You are winning your revolution,' Peter Gzowski wrote. 'In many senses you have already won it. And yet – as though the battle had become more important than the victory – you grow ever more strident. Those of us who have listened to your demands from the outset, and have agreed with your principles, wonder if it isn't time you listened to what *we* have to say, and whether you might want to entertain some principles of

ours, such as the one that nationalism isn't the most important issue in the world of 1964.' That letter is a clear sign
of the times in English Canada; it strongly suggests that
the more radical demands of the French-Canadian nationalists will find little sympathy outside of Quebec.

The most extreme, clear-cut version of the one-nation–
one-vote doctrine is separatism. The supporters of this doctrine reject the view that two nations can live peacefully
in the bosom of a single state. The separatists' counterpart
in English Canada would be assimilationists, who are
nearly, if not completely, non-existent. At present, most
English Canadians would refuse to consider seriously the
possibility of a separate Quebec, and therefore it is nearly
impossible to judge what the response might be if the
majority of Quebeckers opted for independence. Most
English Canadians view the separatists as a rag-tag and
bobtail collection of irresponsible students and people in
or near the criminal fringes of society. At present, nevertheless, there are probably more people in English Canada
who would deplore than applaud the recent bellicose remarks of one English-Canadian historian. Speaking at the
Progressive Conservative Conference on Canadian Goals,
Professor W. L. Morton declared: 'I deny that any province has the right to secede. I think that any such attempt
should be resisted by every means, including force if necessary. . . .' While these remarks may remind some of
the pre-Civil-War years in the United States, they could
equally remind others of the pre-American-Revolution
years in Great Britain!

Many thoughtful French-Canadian nationalists believe
separation would create as many problems as it would
solve. But many of them nevertheless believe that our
polity should be reorganized to give clear recognition to
the 'two nations' theory. In various forms these people have

suggested that a system of 'associate states' should be established, held together by a weak central government in which each nation would be equally represented. English Canada's response to this suggestion has been almost completely negative. The Winnipeg *Free Press* described the proposal as a 'prescription for national suicide', while the Montreal *Star* branded the idea in its various forms as 'half-way houses to separatism'. M. Maurice Lamontagne, a member of the Pearson cabinet from 1963 to 1965 and a man with a broad knowledge of Canadian federalism, told his compatriots quite bluntly that English Canada 'would never negotiate with Quebec a formula of associate states in which the federal government would be reduced to nothing'. He added that in economic terms the idea was completely lacking in realism. In fact, as one French-Canadian wit recently quipped, the theory of 'associate states' might better be called 'co-operative separatism'.

English Canadians are probably quite unprepared to search for solutions to our present problems outside of our present constitutional and political system. At the same time there is a considerable willingness to make modifications within the system. Perhaps this is merely the satisfied conservative's instinctive preference for the familiar; perhaps also it is a realistic reluctance to disturb that precarious balance that has been built up over the years. Still, there is some willingness to modify the balance. Many English Canadians, though probably not a majority, have become convinced that French Canadians have a legitimate claim to better treatment for minority groups outside Quebec. These people, and Professor Morton is among them, favour the extension of bilingualism and biculturalism across the country. This would mean that wherever practical (that is, in terms of numbers of French Canadians), French would become an equal working language in the civil service, a teaching language in minority schools, and even an official language in the courts and legislatures of the provinces. Naturally, most of these improvements would have greater application in New Brunswick, where the French-speaking population is very large, than in British Columbia, where it is tiny.

The major obstacle to these changes is the constitution itself, for education is a provincial matter and will certainly remain one as long as Quebec has any influence in Canadian politics. The provincial politicians whose electorates are largely English-speaking are much less aware of French-Canadian pressures than federal politicians. The truth is, of course, that the French Canadian, though a provincial autonomist, has always received more just treatment from the central government than from the provincial governments. One example of this truism is the Canadian Broadcasting Corporation's autonomous, publicly supported French-language network. The establishment of the French-language radio station CJBC in Toronto recently is a service provided by the federal government that would not have been provided (even if it were constitutionally possible) by the provincial government.

It will be difficult to overcome the reluctance of provincial politicians to grant 'special' rights to French Canadians. One suggestion has been a federal department of education for French- and English-language minorities. On paper the idea is attractive; in practice it is doubtful that either Quebec or the English-speaking provinces would accept it. One group that would certainly accept it is the French-language minorities. It remains to be seen what the Royal Commission on Bilingualism and Biculturalism will have to say on this and other matters. In the meantime, it is worth noting that Ontario and Saskatchewan have to a considerable degree made an effort to place French-language and Roman Catholic minorities in a more equitable position. The situation in New Brunswick, while not perfect, is fairly satisfactory, and there is some hope that Premier Roblin in Manitoba will be able to move his province gradually in a direction more satisfactory to the Franco-Manitobans.

Biculturalism and bilingualism are one thing; decentralization is quite another. At present, decentralization is probably the first item on the agenda of the Quebec government. English Canadians, on the whole, have been brought up to believe that strong central government is a necessity in a country as spread out as Canada. Moreover, there is the completely defensible view that only a strong central government can make the transfer and equalization payments necessary to keep the have-not provinces viable. Therefore decentralization is approached with caution and hostility by many English Canadians. It should be added that rich provinces like British Columbia or Ontario are less concerned about decentralization than poor provinces like Newfoundland or Saskatchewan.

Nevertheless, in their usual stumbling way, Canadians are groping towards an *ad hoc* working arrangement. This pragmatic formula, if it can be given so precise a description, has been dignified by the title of 'co-operative federalism'. The concept was first written into the platform of the New Democratic Party at its founding convention in 1961; it has since been taken over by the Liberal Party. In essence, the formula admits that institutions are less important than practices, and calls for careful and frequent consultations between the various levels of government on an increasingly wide range of policy matters. It places no stock in rewriting the constitution, realizing that the Canadian society is dynamic, not static, and that the present constitution is flexible enough to meet this situation. As one apostle of 'co-operative federalism' recently told a Montreal audience, 'Rewrite the constitution? What an unbelievable waste of time. It is rewritten daily in the facts.'

It may be that this approach will prove too little and too late. Certainly it has been criticized by at least two members of the Lesage government, René Lévesque and Pierre Laporte, as too vague. But it has, in addition to its obvious commitment to careful study of facts and figures rather than heady appeals to rhetoric, one important merit that is not always noticed. That merit is a political one. Realizing that attempts to gauge public opinion in the present unsettled state of Quebec are hopeless, our present federal government has quite rightly chosen to act as though Quebec had only one voice. That voice is the government of Quebec speaking through the Premier, Jean Lesage. And Premier Lesage's latest pronouncement on constitutional matters sounds very like a commitment to the idea of 'co-operative federalism' as it has been expounded by such federal Liberals as MM. Maurice Lamontagne and Jean-Luc Pépin.

On September 28, 1964, Premier Lesage told the Montreal Canadian Club that he did not believe the time was opportune for a full-scale constitutional revision. He went on to state, however, that French Canada had two minimum demands. (No Quebec politician ever states French Canada's maximum, or even intermediate, demands.)

The first of these is a status for the French-speaking Canadian equal in all respects to that of the English-speaking Canadian. This means in the immediate future: French as a working language in the federal administration and French as a teaching language for French minorities outside Quebec. The second claim is that of a genuine decentralization of powers, resources, and decision-making in our federal system. Quebec, I have often said, believes in harmony through consultation and discussion among equals, not through a uniformity imposed by an all-powerful central government. At the moment we believe our political framework to be flexible enough, especially if it were to be adapted to the present circumstances, to allow for a centring in the Quebec government of all the means necessary to the development of a French-Canadian nation mainly concentrated within our borders. This political framework, grounded as it is on historical, geographical, and economic realities, is resilient enough to secure the permanency of a country that stretches from coast to coast.

Premier Lesage may be wrong, though no one as yet has questioned his political sagacity. He may be swept aside in the next rebound of the powerful nationalist tide that is still sweeping Quebec. But in the meantime he is the person who speaks for Quebec. He is the person with whom English Canadians must, and will, co-operate. Of course the success of this pragmatic Pearson-Lesage approach depends on the triumph of reason in both French and English Canada. M. Lesage will have difficulty selling his moderation to some French Canadians, but no more than Mr. Pearson will have with some English Canadians.

For those English Canadians who have attempted to understand the French-Canadian viewpoint, and for those French Canadians who recognize the dangers in the separatist and quasi-separatist siren songs, the future of Canada lies in the construction of a society in which national differences are accepted and where that abstraction 'the nation' is not made the norm of all political, economic, and cultural activity. This is what Claude Ryan, the director of the Montreal nationalist daily *Le Devoir*, has called the 'Canadian hypothesis'. He defined this hypothesis recently, writing that

Canada offers us the chance of constructing a new type of political society, a society whose political boundaries will be advantageous for the development of different cultures without being rigidly or exclusively conditioned by one culture alone. We are convinced that this type of society will reveal itself as more favourable to the cultivation of fundamental liberties, in the long run, than societies calculated too closely on the single reality of a particular culture.

In affirming this conviction we are conscious of enunciating an ideal which is far from having been attained in the Canadian reality. But the difficulties and setbacks of the past have not yet been decisive enough to justify pure and simple abandonment of the ideal which presided at the birth of Confederation.

M. Ryan, in fact, proposes that French and English Canadians exchange Rousseau and Locke for Lord Acton and build a multinational society. It will require a good deal of practical ingenuity to devise the institutions capable of containing the 'Canadian hypothesis'. But our federal system has proven flexible in the past and our politicians are not entirely lacking in the practical skills of political adjustment. And today some of the most thoughtful people in both English and French Canada have recognized the potential value of a Canadian version of the Actonian state. In 1962 Pierre-Elliott Trudeau wrote, in a brilliant analysis of French-Canadian nationalism:

The die is cast in Canada: there are two ethnic and linguistic groups; each is too strong and too deeply rooted in the past, too firmly bound to a mother culture, to be able to swamp the other. But if the two will collaborate inside of a truly pluralist state, Canada could become a privileged place where the federalist form of government, which is the government of tomorrow's world, will be perfected.

More recently, John Holmes, the president of the Canadian Institute of International Affairs, wrote:

One purpose Canada can serve in a world threatened by tribal anarchy is to prove that state and nation are not necessarily coterminous, that people of different cultures and languages can co-exist within a single sovereignty. It is not the same lesson as that of the United States – that divers people can be melted into a successful nation with one official language. Noble as that example has been, it is less applicable than the Canadian experience to new countries which must embrace distinct tribes and clans as founding members within the framework of one effective state.

If there is a solution to the ever-present, but at present critical, problem of the relations between French- and English-speaking Canadians, it must lie in this Actonian direction. Of course, there never will be a perfect or final solution, for the problem is one of human relations. But then there are good reasons, of recent memory, which warn loudly against those who offer a Final Solution.

NINE

The Meaning of Confederation

As the fiftieth anniversary of Confederation approached,
in 1917, a Canadian historian faced with the task of explaining the meaning of Confederation might have concluded that his country's founders intended to build a
nation capable of assisting Great Britain and her allies in
their magnificent effort to make the world safe for democracy. Ten years later, the historian, basking in the glories
of the Balfour Declaration, might well have replied that
the objective of Confederation was to lay the foundations
of a nation capable of winning full autonomy within the
British Commonwealth. Another historian, in the midst of
the Great Depression, would probably have insisted that
the intention of the founders was to establish a nation with
a central government strong enough to guarantee all Canadians a reasonable standard of living and social welfare.
At the end of the Second World War, yet another practi-
tioner of this sensitive craft might have claimed that the
far-seeing statesmen of 1867 had intended to build a nation
capable of interpreting Europe to America, and vice versa.
A decade ago the answer would certainly have been that
the great object of Confederation was to build a nation in
the northern half of the North American continent strong

enough to resist annexation to the United States. Perhaps in the 1970s some particularly perceptive reader of the *Confederation Debates* will be able to conclude that the real intention of those serious, if not always sober, Victorian gentlemen who sat around the tables at Charlottetown, Quebec, and London was to build a nation scientific enough to launch a bilingual astronaut on his travels to the moon.

Each of those historians, it should be noted, would be English-speaking. A French-speaking historian would in some cases have given those same answers. But he would also have insisted that there was another objective equal to if not prior to the ones emphasized by his English-speaking colleagues. The French-speaking historian would have maintained, at each of the dates mentioned, that the objective of Confederation was to guarantee the survival of *la nation canadienne-française.* He would then have gone on either to defend or to criticize Confederation according to his view of how fully this objective had been served.*

While each of these interpretations, in its French and English variations, is based with a greater or lesser degree of accuracy, the answer of the mid 1960s must place the emphasis on yet another interpretation. This interpretation stems from the most permanent theme in Canadian history: the relations between French- and English-speaking Canadians. Among the several objectives of the architects of the Canadian constitution, none was more important than the effort to accommodate the needs of the two cultural

---

*French-Canadian historians have not written much of a scholarly kind about Confederation, but two rather different approaches can be found in Lionel Groulx, *La Confédération canadienne* (Montreal, 1918), and Thomas Chapais, *Cours d'histoire du Canada* (Quebec, 1934), Vol. VIII.

communities that had been made co-inhabitants of British North America by the Seven Years' War and the American Revolution. In the minds of the men of 1867, that accommodation was to be achieved by the founding of a new nation. But the important question relates to their definition of the form of that nation.

Several years ago a young French-Canadian intellectual began his explanation of his position as a Quebec separatist with some lines that go directly to the heart of the meaning of the word 'nation' in the context of Confederation. In his tract *J'ai choisi l'indépendance*, Raymond Barbeau wrote:

> The national thought of French Canadians has always seemed ambiguous to me; most of those who defend our interests remain undecided before the following question: does the French-Canadian nation exist? According to the response that we give, our political and patriotic activity will be centred on the state of Quebec or, inversely, on Canada and the federal government. If the Canadian 'nation' exists, the French-Canadian 'nation' has never existed, or exists no longer, either in theory or in practice.

That claim represents the fundamental assumption of the separatist thesis in the current debate over the future of Confederation. It is that a nation must express itself through a sovereign state. A nation that lacks a state of its own is a colony and therefore must, like other colonies, win its independence.

The view that state and nation must be coterminous represents a form of political orthodoxy that finds its roots in the French Revolution, was nurtured by the accidental alliance of liberals and nationalists in the nineteenth century, and flowered under the warm sun of Wilsonianism at Versailles in 1919. That the plant has now clearly produced bitter, even poisonous, fruit has not greatly decreased its apparently habit-forming attractions. Indeed, in the 1960s ideological nationalism, with its emphasis on cultural homogeneity and the right of self-determination, is perhaps more alive and more inebriating than at any time since 1848.

Yet despite the nineteenth-century origins of what is perhaps best called the ideal of the nationalist-state, it was a different ideal that motivated the founders of the Canadian nation. That is why any answer to the question of the meaning of Confederation must be both exceedingly simple and extremely complex. If it were just one or the other we would almost certainly not have had that apparently endless search for the elusive Canadian identity, and French-Canadian identity, which has characterized so much writing about Canada. Nor would we have had the ever-repeating debate about the functions of the various levels of government in Canada if the men of 1864-7 had given us a statement of intention either so simple that every schoolboy could grasp it or so complex that only a philosopher-king could interpret it. But Sir John A. Macdonald's merry men did neither. Hence the debate and hence also the fascination of Canadian history.

The meaning of Confederation was, first, simple. There cannot be the slightest doubt that the intention of the Fathers of Confederation was, in Macdonald's words, the 'founding of a great nation'. Here on the northern half of the North American continent 'a new nationality' was being founded. Not one of the supporters of the scheme, English- or French-speaking, contended otherwise. The opponents of the scheme, from whatever part of British North America they came, recognized the nation-building objective of the proposals. For various reasons they thought that the new nation was either impractical or undesirable or both.

· But what kind of a nation could be built out of four or five scattered colonies which knew either too little about one another, as was the case of the Maritimes and Canada, or too much about one another, as was the case of Canada East (as Quebec was then called) and Canada West (later Ontario)? It is in answering this question that the original-ity and deviationism of the founders of Canada become clear and the complexity of the problem becomes obvious. While the Fathers of Confederation were intent upon estab-lishing a 'nation-state', they were equally forthright in their rejection of the ideal of the 'nationalist-state'. The nation whose foundations were being laid was not culturally ho-mogeneous. Nor was it the objective of the politicians of the Great Coalition to build a structure that would enforce or produce ultimate homogeneity. In the house of the Fathers of Confederation there were to be many mansions. In explaining why he had forsaken his ideal of a single, uni-tary legislative union in favour of a federal system, Mac-donald, who understood every detail of the scheme, had this to say:

In the first place it [legislative union] would not have met the assent of the people of Lower Canada, because they felt that in their peculiar position – being a minority with a different lan-guage, nationality and religion from the majority – in case of a junction with the other provinces, their institutions and their laws might be assailed, and their ancestral associations, on which they prided themselves, attacked and prejudiced; it was found that any proposition which involved the absorption of the individuality of Lower Canada – if I may use the expression – would not be re-ceived with favour by her people.

Macdonald, who had successfully trod through the no-man's-land of sectional, religious, and cultural quarrels for twenty years before Confederation, knew that the key to political success and constitutional stability was har-mony between French and English Canadians. He defined his formula in 1856 when he told an English-speaking Montrealer: 'Treat them [the French Canadians] as a nation and they will act as a free people generally do –

generously. Call them a faction and they become factious.'

But how could one build a 'nation' and yet treat the French Canadians as a 'nation'? Macdonald supplied his answer in the Confederation debates. The British constitutional system was one that required no enforced uniformity, but rather provided for the protection of minority rights. 'We will enjoy here', Macdonald claimed, 'the great test of constitutional freedom – we will have the rights of the minority respected.' This point was explained more fully by George Etienne Cartier, the leading French Canadian among the Fathers. Cartier was naturally very sensitive to the charge made by his opponents that the much-talked-about 'new nationality' would engulf the French-Canadian nationality. Had not Lord Durham been one of the first to propose federation of all British North America? And for what purpose? None other than to erase the French-Canadian nation from the face of British North America. Cartier made it plain, however, that the nation whose birth he was attending would be the very antithesis of the Anglo-Saxon nationalism that Durham had supported:

Now when we were united together, if union were attained, we would form a political nationality with which neither national origin, nor the religion of any individual would interfere. . . . In our federation we should have Catholic and Protestant, English, French, Irish, Scotch, and each in his efforts and success would increase the prosperity and glory of our new Confederacy.

Thus while it is true that in 1867 the political leaders of Canada were engaged in that characteristic nineteenth-century activity, the building of a nation-state, it is likewise true, and highly significant, that they were rejecting that equally characteristic nineteenth-century phenomenon, the nationalist-state. Their concept of Canada was of a community based on political and juridical unity, but

also on cultural and religious duality. And the key to that
unity in duality was the rejection of the intolerant, conformist, ideological nationalism that was, in these same
years, shaking the foundations of Europe and also providing the drive that led to the destruction of the Southern
Confederacy by the North in the American Civil War.

The second key to the meaning of Confederation was
that the new union was to be a federal one. In this fashion,
diversity was to be given specific institutional guarantees.
Federalism, as has often been remarked, was not a very
well understood system of government in the nineteenth
century.* And where it was known, in the United States, it
did not provide a very encouraging example. Yet federalism was indispensable if there was to be a union of British
North America. The Maritime Provinces were quite unwilling to be completely absorbed into the upstart culture
of Canada. More important, the French Canadians refused
to give up the relative security of the union where Canada
East and Canada West enjoyed equal representation for a
new union based on representation by population unless
they were given the means of protecting their individuality.
Arthur Gordon, the Governor of New Brunswick, watched
the preliminary discussions on the projected union and
reported to the Colonial Secretary, 'The aim of Lower
Canada is a local independence as complete as circumstances will permit, and the peculiarities of race, religion
and habits which distinguish its people render their desire
respectable and natural.' And when Lord Carnarvon, the
Colonial Secretary, presented the British North America

---

*For an account of federal ideas in Canada, see Peter B. Waite, *The
Life and Times of Confederation* (Toronto, 1962), and Jean-Charles
Bonenfant, 'L'Idée que les Canadiens français de 1864 pouvaient
avoir du fédéralisme', *Culture*, Vol. XXV, December 4, 1964, pages
307-22.

Act to the House of Lords in February 1867 he noted that 'Lower Canada now *consents* to enter into this Confederation because its peculiar institutions were to be given effective guarantees.' The great compromise of 1867, and at the same time the great victory for the French Canadians, was the federal system of government. Had there been only one 'nation' involved in the negotiations that preceded the establishment of Confederation, the proponents of legislative union would doubtless have fought harder for their viewpoint. Since there was not one nation but two, the result was federalism.

What is perhaps not often enough emphasized in discussions of Confederation is that while the events of 1864 to 1867 produced a union, they also produced a division. From 1841 to 1865 Canada East and Canada West had been united in a theoretically unitary, but practically federal, state. The experience had been less than satisfying. Moreover, it was not only, or even chiefly, the French Canadians who were anxious to bring this unhappy condition to an end. Indeed, throughout the last years of the union the loudest complaints came from the Liberals in Canada West. Led by George Brown, the Grit party practically made its fortune on two cries: 'French domination' and 'rep by pop'. The federal system adopted in 1867 provided the means whereby this so-called French domination could be ended and representation by population implemented with the approval of the French Canadians. This explains the exuberant tone of the letter George Brown scribbled to his wife at the end of the Quebec Conference in 1864. 'All right!!' he whooped. 'Confederation through at six o'clock this evening – constitution adopted – a creditable document – a complete reform of all the abuses and injustices we have complained of! Is it not wonderful? French Canadianism entirely extinguished.' That last line about 'French Canadianism' speaks volumes about the history of the United Canadas! In the debates that took place in the Parliament of the Canadas on the subject of the Quebec Resolutions, speaker after speaker, in more restrained terms than the editor of the Toronto *Globe*, noted that the proposed Confederation was 'a separation of the provinces', as the venerable Sir E. P. Taché put it. Once more the complexity of Confederation is obvious: to unity in duality has been added unity in separation.

To the English-speaking Fathers, unity was all-important. Macdonald repeatedly emphasized his preference for a legislative union – which he evidently thought was compatible with cultural duality. Each of the supporters of the scheme emphasized the necessity of a strong central government if the new nation-state was to survive in the face of a rapidly changing world. In the newly emerging balance of world power, Britain seemed anxious to retreat from her costly commitments in North America at a time when the United States, the traditional enemy of British North America, was giving proof of its enormous military strength. Both French and English supporters of the Confederation scheme were agreed that a central government capable of initiating effective military and economic policies was necessary if British North America was to survive. Every nation is founded on a will to survive. Canada was no exception and it was that will which united French- and English-speaking British North Americans in 1867. In 1940 the report of a royal commission, the Rowell-Sirois Commission, which had been appointed to carry out a full-scale examination of the Canadian federal system, made the point in this way:

Confederation was conceived as a solution for a number of political and economic difficulties and, therefore, had both political and economic aims. Politically it was designed to establish a new nation to meet the changed conditions of British policy and to brace the scattered provinces against possible American aggression. Economically it was intended to foster a national economy which would relieve dependence upon a few industries and lessen exposure to the effects of the economic policies pursued by the United States and Great Britain.

With these objectives in mind, the men who drafted the British North America Act placed the preponderance of power, including the residual power, in the hands of the central government.*

So broad were the powers of the proposed central government, the critics of the scheme charged that to describe the system as federal was to divest the term of all known meaning. 'I am opposed to the scheme of Confederation,' Eric Dorion, the *enfant terrible* of French Canada, announced, 'because the first resolution is nonsense and repugnant to truth; it is not a federal union which is offered, but a legislative union in disguise.' The fear that disturbed these French-Canadian opponents of the plan was quite simple: had the Macdonalds and Cartiers, in their concern for Canadian survival, produced a system of government that would threaten *la survivance de la nation canadienne-française*? Cartier, of course, said no; but his response failed to convince a significant number of his compatriots.†

---

*Today even French Canadians appear to accept this view of the intention of the Fathers, though traditionally they have been loath to do so. (See Jean-Charles Bonenfant, 'L'Esprit de 1867', *Revue d'histoire de l'Amérique française*, Vol. XVII, No. 1, June 1963, pages 19-38.)

†It is, of course, impossible to know the exact strength of the opposition to Confederation since the matter was not put to a popular test. One French-Canadian writer, after a less than exhaustive analysis, has concluded that a majority of French Canadians probably supported the scheme. (See Jean-Charles Bonenfant, 'Les Canadiens français et la naissance de la Confédération', *Report of the Canadian Historical Association*, 1952, page 45.)

This sharp difference of opinion is another reminder of the duality of the country and also of the duality of the motives that lay behind the union of 1867. Therefore, just as the Rowell-Sirois Report stressed the theme of Canadian survival as the central factor in Confederation, a Quebec royal commission in 1956, the Tremblay Commission, stressed the factor of French-Canadian survival. And just as the Rowell-Sirois Commission emphasized the centralized character of the 1867 scheme, so the Tremblay Commission underlined provincial powers. Here is the way the Quebec commissioners concluded their consideration of the events of 1864-7:

To sum up, the Union of 1867 met the common needs of the provinces. If it assumed a federative character it was doubtless due to their divergencies, but it was especially due to the irreducible presence of the French Canadian bloc which only accepted Confederation because it had been given every conceivable promise that it would be able to govern itself in autonomous fashion and thereby develop, along with all its institutions, according to its special way of life and its own culture.

Those who try to read orthodox nationalist assumptions into Confederation – that is to say, those who argue that Canada is a nationalist-state rather than a nation-state – always fail to realize that survival and *la survivance* are not necessarily interchangeable words. Indeed, rather than being interchangeable, the two realities that the words represent are in a constant state of tension. It was one of the fundamental objectives of the Fathers of Confederation to bring that tension into a state of equilibrium. Confederation was an agreement, pact, or *entente*, whichever of those words best describes the political rather·than the legal character of the events of 1864-7. And the terms of that *entente* were that a new nation-state was to be founded on the basis of an acceptance of cultural duality and on a division of powers. The unstated major premise of that *entente* was that both survival and *la survivance* were legitimate objectives and that those objectives could better be achieved within the structure of a single, federal state than in separate states or in a unitary state. The unceasing responsibility of Canadian political leaders since 1867 has been to ensure that the equilibrium between survival and *la survivance*, between the legitimate goals of Canadians and of French Canadians, should not be destroyed. It has never been an easy assignment.

There can be no doubt that a homogeneous nation is more easily governed than one based on cultural duality, though the history of the American federal system, especially before 1865, stands as a constant warning against easy generalization. But in Canada cultural duality adds a second type of potential friction to that inherent in any polity organized on federal lines. Within the Canadian federal system there have been, in general terms, three types of conflict. Each of these conflicts has involved the problem of cultural duality; but two of them have also been entangled in the question of divided jurisdiction.

The first type of conflict has arisen as part of the struggle for political power at Ottawa. There is always a danger, in a society composed of diverse cultural and religious elements, that an ambitious or frustrated politician will attempt to build his fortunes on stimulating antagonism rather than on conciliating differences. On the whole, Canada has been remarkably free of this type of politician. Nearly all of our leaders seem to have realized that party lines must not be allowed to coincide with national lines. Such a party division would be especially dangerous for French Canadians. 'Why, so soon as the French Canadians, who are in a minority in this country, were to organize as a political party, they would compel the majority to organize as a political party and the result would be disastrous to themselves,' Wilfrid Laurier warned in 1886. Theoretically, as a Conservative tactician argued as recently as 1956, it is possible for a party to win power by appealing exclusively to English Canada. But even if English Canadians were united enough to be herded into the same political corral, it is doubtful if successful government could be carried on.*

On at least two occasions a complete French-English division has nearly been reached. These crises, in 1917 and 1942, both centred on the question of conscription for overseas service, which the vast majority of French Canadians opposed and most English Canadians favoured. But in general Canadian federal parties have served the country well in their role of finding a working consensus in a culturally divided country. Their weakness is that they must be parties of compromise, and compromise can sometimes become an excuse for the evasion of responsibility. That is why our party system has most often, in the twentieth century, been a multi-party system composed of one or more major 'parties of consensus' and several 'parties of principle or interest'. The latter type of party has never gained power in Canada, but if one did it would almost certainly be rapidly transformed into a party of consensus. The 'price of union' in Canada appears to be parties of compromise and consensus.

A second type of conflict that has produced serious national friction has grown out of the question of the rights of French Canadians living outside of Quebec. While both French and English were made official languages in the

*John Meisel, *The Canadian General Election of 1957* (Toronto, 1962). The tactician, Gordon Churchill, added significantly: 'The statement is frequently made that "you cannot govern the country without Quebec" and to this statement there is no serious disagreement, for in the interests of national unity all parts of Canada should be represented in the government.'

federal parliament, the British North America Act made no special provision for the French language or French schools outside of Quebec – though the Protestant, English-speaking minority was well provided for inside Quebec. It is true that some protection was provided for religious minorities outside of Quebec, and perhaps the Fathers assumed that their successors would be as liberal as themselves in allowing both religious and national minorities equality of rights. The hope, if it existed, proved too optimistic.

By its very intention, Confederation was expansionist. It was to provide the answer to American 'manifest destiny' which threatened to absorb parts of mid-western and far-western British North America. As George Brown, the voice of Ontario manifest destiny, put it, 'What we propose now is but to lay the foundations of the structure – to set in motion the governmental machinery that will one day, we trust, extend from the Atlantic to the Pacific.' The Confederation scheme could not be completed without this commitment to expansion; it was a necessary element in the over-all pattern of British North American survival. Yet it was also a threat to the new Confederation – just as Western expansion threatened the American federal system before 1860, for western settlement would inevitably raise the question of the rights of French Canada's 'peculiar institutions'. The question was especially difficult since these territories would almost certainly be filled with non-French-speaking settlers. There were those French Canadians who recognized the danger early and appealed to Quebec to send colonists to Manitoba 'in the interests of our future influence in Confederation'. But the appeal went largely unheeded. French-language rights had been recognized in both Manitoba in 1870 and the Northwest Territories in 1875, but these privileges were largely swept away by the end of the century. The privileges were abolished by people who accepted the view of the Ontario member of parliament who told the House of Commons in 1890: 'I say that we have not, that we cannot have and never will have in this country, two nationalities.' It was the belief of such people as these, as D'Alton McCarthy put it at Stayner, Ontario, in 1889, that 'This is a British country, and the sooner we take up our French Canadians and make them British, the less trouble will we leave for posterity.' What these people really wanted was to replace the Canadian nation-state, based on cultural duality, with a Canadian nationalist-state based on a uniform British-Canadian culture.

'McCarthyism', as it might well be called, insisted that Canada was a British country by right of conquest, and that it could only become a real nation if that right of conquest was used to create cultural homogeneity. Sir John Macdonald rejected these claims completely and in so doing once more defined his view of the meaning of Confederation:

I have no accord with the desire expressed in some quarters that by any mode whatever there should be an attempt made to oppress the one language or to render it inferior to the other; I believe that it would be impossible if it were tried, and it would be foolish and wicked if it were possible. The statement that has been made so often that this is a conquered country is *à propos de rien*. Whether it was conquered or ceded, we have a constitution now under which all British subjects are in a position of absolute equality, having equal rights of every kind – of language, of religion, of property, and of person. There is no paramount race in this country, there is no conquered race in this country; we are all British subjects, and those who are not English are none the less British on that account.

In 1890 Macdonald had only a little more than a year to live. The theory of equality expressed in his defence of the French language in the Northwest did not live much longer. As the immigrants flocked to the empty plains from all parts of Europe and the United States, the French-speaking minority was rapidly outnumbered. Once more that most difficult of all problems of democracy was raised: the relation of minority rights to majority rule. Mgr Taché, the ecclesiastical and national leader of the French Canadians in Manitoba, foresaw the outcome. 'Number is going to make us weak,' he wrote, 'and since under our constitutional system number is power, we are going to find ourselves at the mercy of those who do not love us.'

First in Manitoba in the nineties, and then in the new provinces of Saskatchewan and Alberta in 1905, the privileges of the French and Catholic minority were reduced to a minimum. The arguments against minority schools were chiefly of two kinds. One arose from an intense Protestantism or, perhaps better, an intense anti-Catholicism. John Willison, the distinguished editor of the Toronto *News*, explained his hostility to separate schools in 1905 when he wrote to Sir Wilfrid Laurier: 'While I have all this respect and consideration for the natural race sentiment of French Canadians no man could be more strenuously opposed to clerical interference in state affairs. And from Confederation down the plain meaning of the constitution has been deliberately perverted to serve the ends of the Roman Catholic hierarchy.' In those years, to argue against separate schools was to argue against French schools.

The second argument was, in effect, that unless English was made the sole language of all the schools in the West, a Canadian 'nation' could never emerge from the polyglot western population. This view had a natural attraction on the prairies, and the patriotic fervour created by the First World War provided the necessary heat to set the melting-pot boiling. That process, like many experiments in mass-produced uniformity, had first been tested in the United States. Its Canadian version rarely distinguished between recent immigrants from Poland and French-speaking Manitobans whose ancestors had arrived in North America in the seventeenth or eighteenth centuries. The process was well illustrated in Manitoba. In 1916, when bilingual schools were finally and completely abolished, a Franco-Manitoban protested in the legislature that 'the French are a distinctive race, and will not be assimilated whether you like it or not'. To this *cri de coeur* a cabinet minister of Icelandic origin replied: 'I want those who agree with that statement to consider what would happen if all the nationalities represented in this province were to adopt that attitude. What kind of a Manitoba would we have a hundred years from now?' The attitude here expressed was that the Franco-Manitobans were a minority like any other minority, and must therefore be cast into the Manitoba melting-pot.

Yet this view was not accepted by all the Western provinces. In 1918, when Saskatchewan made certain modifications in its school laws in order to 'nationalize' its ethnic minorities, a small exception was made for the French-speaking group – though only after a cabinet minister had resigned in protest against an initial plan to homogenize all the minorities. In the debate, one minister of the Saskatchewan government who knew his country's history better than his Manitoba colleague told the legislature: 'Saskatchewan is an integral part of our Dominion. Confederation came as the result of a compromise for the sake of unity. French was the official language of the Dominion and because we have the legislative power to wipe it out I cannot see the justification for violating the principle upon which Confederation unity was founded, just because we have that power.'

It is nevertheless true that increasingly in English Canada the principle of majority rule took precedence over minority rights. Macdonald's tolerant belief that there were at least two ways of being Canadian was replaced by a rigid, even intolerant, adherence to the letter of the British North America Act. John W. Dafoe, a leading exponent of Canadian nationalism, exemplified this new rigidity. Annoyed by some criticisms that a French-Canadian friend levelled at the unilingual Manitoba school system, Dafoe retorted:

You have allowed yourself to become committed to the theory that the Dominion of Canada, as a whole, is a bilingual country in every portion of which the French have precisely the same rights as the English. Canada is not, however, a bilingual country, either by treaty, or in law, or in fact, and you cannot establish that it is by either of the courses open to you: an appeal to the law courts or an appeal to the court of public opinion.

By the strict letter of the law, Dafoe was quite correct. But by insisting on that strict view and backing it up with a scarcely veiled appeal to the tyranny of the democratic majority, he was rejecting the essential spirit of Confederation. 'In all countries the rights of the majority take care of themselves,' Macdonald had remarked in 1865, 'but it is only in countries like England, enjoying constitutional liberty, and safe from the tyranny of a single despot *or of an unbridled democracy*, that the rights of minorities are regarded.'

Dafoe's nationalism, founded on a firm belief in 'unbridled democracy', was accepted as the standard by most English Canadians. Only a man with the optimism of Henri Bourassa, the founder of the Montreal nationalist daily *Le Devoir*, could maintain his faith in a Canadian nation founded on a genuine dualism. In 1928 he again expressed this primary article in his political creed, which he called 'nationalism', in a letter to one of the many unconverted, J. W. Dafoe:

Most of us are sincerely and profoundly convinced that the federal pact was based on the recognition of a perfect equality of rights as between English-speaking and French-speaking Canadians, and also as between Catholics and Protestants, in all matters relating to education, whether religious or linguistic. And in this as you know we have the solemn word and testimony of Sir John Macdonald himself. We not less sincerely believe that Confederation cannot endure and Canada obtain her full destiny as a nation, unless this broad principle of dualism obtains everywhere.

To quote that statement is to measure the gulf that divided two Canadian nationalists and probably the two most influential Canadian journalists of the twentieth century.

A third type of conflict in Canada is one familiar to every inhabitant of a federal polity. It is the conflict between federal and provincial authorities. The history of federal-provincial friction in Canada is as old as Confederation itself, and it has never been simply a clash between Ottawa and Quebec. Indeed some of the most vigorous exponents of provincial rights have been English-Canadian provincial leaders. Oliver Mowat of Ontario is the grandfather of them all. His attacks on the federal power in the eighties were followed by those of Sir Richard McBride of British Columbia in the early years of this century, Howard Ferguson and Mitchell Hepburn of Ontario in the twenties and thirties, William Aberhart of Alberta and T. D. Pattullo of British Columbia in the thirties, and George Drew of Ontario and Angus L. Macdonald of Nova Scotia in the late forties and early fifties.

Nevertheless the struggle for provincial autonomy has had a particular meaning and appeal for French Canadians. Every premier of Quebec, from Honoré Mercier in the 1880s down to Jean Lesage today, has at least paid lip-service to provincial rights, and more often has carried on a running conflict with Ottawa. Indeed, the most serious threat to the original concept of Confederation as a nation-state founded on cultural duality has always been the possibility that some day French Canadians would come to identify their nation solely with the provincial state. One of the most serious results of the limitations that were placed on the rights of French Canadians outside Quebec has been the growing feeling that only Quebec was the 'national-state' of French Canada. This process of 'nationalizing' the provincial state began in the eighties, shortly after Quebeckers were shocked to discover that their delegation at Ottawa had been unable to prevent the execution of Louis Riel, the Métis leader of two Western rebellions. But the pace has gathered momentum in the age of industrialization and urbanization, since both phenomena have raised serious questions about traditional political jurisdictions. The fact that Quebec was industrialized largely by 'foreign' capital stimulated the French Canadians' national consciousness. Moreover the development took place during a period when French Canadians, as a result of their unhappy memories of 1917 and their fears of a new world war, were exceedingly suspicious of the federal authority. That, in part, explains the fact that while many English Canadians have since the Great Depression demanded increased federal involvement in social welfare, economic development, and education programs, most French Canadians have resisted federal largess even when it meant forgoing the kind of welfare-state policies that make life livable in modern society.

Perhaps the key point in this development was the election in 1936 of Premier Maurice Duplessis and his Union Nationale party. For the first time, a party held office in Quebec that had no federal affiliations. It was a specifically provincial party and, as its name suggested, it identified the nation with the province – despite the fact that its leaders paid homage occasionally to the idea of a bicultural or bi-national Canada. Thus began a period when French Canadians looked more and more to their provincial government as the primary defender of *la survivance*. This development took place at the very time when English Canadians were becoming convinced that Canadian survival depended on a more active central government. That is the crux of our present discontents.

During the 1950s English Canadians became rapidly aware of the vulnerability of their small nation alone in North America with the giant United States. Survival seemed more than ever to depend on a federal government capable of implementing new national policies in the economic, social, and cultural fields that would strengthen Canadian individuality and independence.* French Canadians, no less fearful of the all-pervasive influence of the United States, reacted coolly, even with hostility, to many of the new national panaceas. Typical is the comment of a French-Canadian nationalist on the *Report of the Royal Commission on National Development in the Arts, Letters and Sciences*, better known as the Massey Report. 'When the Massey Report registers the dangers of the American way of life, it sees accurately,' he wrote. 'When it brings its support to the centralizing movement, it opts for a bad remedy. For one can never assure the defence of Canada when one contributes to the dismantling of one of its bastions.' What worried French Canadians in the 1950s, as it had worried them a century earlier, was that an all-powerful central government might become the instrument, not

*For the standard argument, see the *Report of the Royal Commission on Broadcasting* (Ottawa, 1957), page 9. The same argument underlies both the Massey Commission report (1951), and the O'Leary Commission report (1963).

of duality, but of a homogeneous nationalism that would stifle the minority. The fear was expressed in an extreme form by a group who declared: 'Those who pretend to work for the formation of a single nation called "Canada" desire, consciously or unconsciously, the complete assimilation of the weaker nation by the stronger.'

By the beginning of the 1960s many French Canadians had begun to question the validity of the Confederation concept. At the basis of these questions is the belief that the *entente* of 1867 has been broken, that tension between survival and *la survivance* has mounted to a final crisis. 'Canada is a reality whose very existence is only possible by the coexistence of two antagonisms,' a young radical separatist wrote recently. If there is antagonism rather than cooperation, it is because the meaning of Confederation has become blurred. That meaning was that two nations could survive and grow inside a single nation-state, provided each nation refrained from claiming an exclusively nationalist-state. The *entente* of 1867 was based on the belief that the federal government would be the instrument of both survival and *la survivance*. The provinces, of course, also had a role to play. But if they, or even one of them, ever fully assumed responsibility for one of the components of the 'new nation', then the *entente* would be a failure.

Today the experiment is by no means over. But no one can doubt that it is passing through a period of profound readjustment. If the original, imaginative concept of Confederation cannot be reshaped to meet the needs of today's Canada, then, as a wise French Canadian has recently observed, 'the blind forces of national pride will be let loose for good'. At that point the meaning of Confederation will be finally destroyed, for it will mark the triumph of nationalism over the nation-state.

Notes

INTRODUCTION

Page Line

5   3   Henri Bourassa, *Le Patriotisme canadien-français* (Montreal, 1902), page 14.

      7   George Orwell, 'Notes on Nationalism', in *Such, Such Were the Joys* (New York, 1953), page 75.

      13   Elie Kedourie, *Nationalism* (London, 1960).

      30   Lord Acton, 'Nationality', in *Essays on Freedom and Power* (New York, 1955), pages 160-9.

CANADA AND THE FRENCH-CANADIAN QUESTION

6   14   André Laurendeau in *Le Devoir*, January 5, 1963.

7   6   Bruce Hutchison, *Mr. Prime Minister, 1867-1964* (Toronto, 1964), page xi.

9   11   Jean-Noël Tremblay, M.P. See *Canadian Annual Review* for 1961 (Toronto, 1962), page 90.

Page Line
12   26   Pierre Vadeboncoeur, 'A Break with Tradi-
             tion?', *Queen's Quarterly*, Vol. LXV, No. 1,
             Spring 1958, page 92.

14   15   *Le Devoir*, July 5, 1963.

16   31   Frank Scott and Michael Oliver, *Quebec
             States Her Case* (Toronto, 1964), page 30.

18   12   Albert Breton, 'The Economics of National-
             ism', *Journal of Political Economy*, Vol.
             LXXII, No. 4, August 1964, pages 376-86.

      29   See, for example, André Major, 'Arms in
             Hand', in Scott and Oliver, *op. cit.*, pages
             73-82.

19   22   Scott and Oliver, pages 152-6. Jean Mar-
             chand is now an M.P. and a former member
             of the Royal Commission on Bilingualism
             and Biculturalism.

20   19   Gérard Pelletier, 'Profil d'un démagogue',
             Cité libre, 14th year, No. 53, January 1963.

22   32   Maurice Lamontagne, speech to the Club
             Richelieu de Québec, September 9, 1964.

25   13   *Le Devoir*, July 5, 1963.

      25   W. L. Morton, 'Clio in Canadian History',
             University of Toronto Quarterly, Vol. XV,
             No. 3, April 1946, page 234.

QUEBEC, ONTARIO, AND THE NATION

28   18   *Proceedings of the Reform Convention held
             at Toronto on the 27th and 28th of June,
             1867* (Toronto, 1867).

      34   Sir Joseph Pope, *The Correspondence of Sir
             John Macdonald* (Toronto, 1920), page 75.

29   10   J. C. Morrison, *Oliver Mowat and the De-*

Page	Line	
		velopment of Provincial Rights in Ontario: A Study in Dominion Provincial Relations, 1867-1896, published by the Ontario Department of Public Records and Archives.
30	22	See, for example, 'The Interprovincial Resolutions Debate', Toronto *Globe*, March 9, 1888.
31	7	*Dominion-Provincial Conference, 1941* (Ottawa, 1941), page 80.
32	25	*Le Devoir*, September 16, 1965.
33	7	J. M. S. Careless, 'The Toronto *Globe* and Agrarian Radicalism', *Canadian Historical Review*, Vol. XXIX, No. 1, March 1948, pages 14-40.
	12	Toronto *Globe*, June 2, 1869.
	19	W. L. Morton, *Manitoba: A History* (Toronto, 1957).
34	5	R. O. Macfarlane, 'Manitoba Politics and Parties after Confederation', *Report of the Canadian Historical Association, 1940*, pages 45-55.
35	18	Toronto *Saturday Night*, March 1905.
	28	Armand Lavergne, *Les Ecoles du Nord-Ouest* (Montreal, 1907), page 18.
36	22	Toronto *Evening Telegram*, August 2, 1888.
	23	Franklin Walker, *Catholic Education and Politics in Ontario* (Toronto, 1964), pages 126-57.
37	6	*Orange Sentinel*, February 3, 1910.
	24	*Canadian Annual Review, 1916* (Toronto, 1917), page 34.
38	34	Canada, *House of Commons Debates, 1927*, page 824.

Page Line
39   18   *Ibid.*, pages 825-6.
41   32   George J. McNair, 'Montreal: Key to Que-
            bec's Place in the Sun', Toronto *Globe and
            Mail*, October 1, 1965, page B5.
42   29   J. W. Dafoe, 'The Problems of Canada', in
            Cecil B. Hurst, *Great Britain and the Do-
            minions* (Chicago, 1928), pages 175-6.

QUEBEC AND CONFEDERATION: PAST AND PRESENT

44   9   Sir Joseph Pope (ed.), *Confederation, Being
            a Series of hitherto unpublished Documents
            Bearing on the British North America Act*
            (Toronto, 1895).
      17   A. G. Doughty, 'Notes on the Quebec Confer-
            ence, 1864', *Canadian Historical Review*,
            Vol. I, No. 1, March 1920, page 28.
45   5   *Parliamentary Debates on the Subject of the
            Confederation of the British North American
            Provinces* (Quebec, 1965) (hereafter cited
            as *Confederation Debates*), page 368.
47   2   *Ibid.*, page 711. On 'biculturalism' and Con-
            federation, see Eugene Forsey, 'The British
            North America Act and Biculturalism',
            Queen's Quarterly, Vol. LXXI, No. 2, Sum-
            mer 1964, pages 141-9.
48   16   Charles Langelier, *Souvenirs politiques*
            (Montreal, 1909), Vol. I, page 254.
49   4   T. J. J. Loranger, *Letters on the Interpreta-
            tion of the Federal Constitution called the
            British North America Act* (Quebec, 1884)
            (first letter), page 61. In 1884, as leader of
            the Opposition in Quebec, Mercier used

Page Line

Loranger's writings as a source for a speech on provincial autonomy. See J. O. Pelland, *Biographie, discours, conférences, etc., de l'hon. Honoré Mercier* (Montreal, 1890), page 401.

50   31   Sir Wilfrid Laurier, 'Le Fédéralisme', *Revue trimestrielle canadienne*, November 1918, pages 219-21.

51   9   Edmond de Nevers, *L'Avenir du peuple canadien-français* (Paris, 1896), page 293.

      19   Canada, *House of Commons Debates, 1890*, Vol. I, page 745.

      32   Henri Bourassa, *La Conscription* (Montreal, 1917), page 20.

52   11   Jean-Charles Falardeau, 'Les Canadiens français et leur idéologie', in Mason Wade (ed.), *Canadian Dualism* (Toronto, 1960), page 25.

      28   Jules-Paul Tardivel, *Pour la patrie* (Montreal, 1895), page 7.

53   7   Dosteler O'Leary, *Séparatisme, doctrine constructif* (Montreal, 1937), page 150; Emile Latrémouille, *Tradition et indépendance* (Montreal, 1939), pages 28-9.

      34   *Quebec and Confederation. A Record of the Debate of the Legislative Assembly of Quebec on the Motion proposed by J.-N. Francoeur* (Quebec, 1918), page 124.

54   33   H. F. Quinn, *The Union Nationale* (Toronto, 1963), cited pages 117-18.

55   19   André Laurendeau, *La Crise de la conscription, 1942* (Montreal, 1962), page 74. See *L'Action nationale*, Vol. XIX, No. 1, January 1942, pages 48-50.

Page Line
22   F.-A. Angers, 'Un Vote de race', *L'Action nationale*, Vol. XIX, No. 4, May 1942, pages 299-313.

26   R. McG. Dawson, *The Conscription Crisis of 1944* (Toronto, 1961), and André Laurendeau, *La Crise de la conscription*.

56   7   *La Crise de la conscription*, page 152.

19   'Mémoire de la Ligue d'Action Nationale à la Commission royale d'enquête sur les arts, les lettres et les sciences', *L'Action nationale*, Vol. XXXV, No. 4, April 1950, page 312; see also Michel Brunet, 'Une autre manifestation du nationalisme Canadian, le Rapport Massey', in *Canadians et Canadiens* (Montreal, 1952).

29   André Laurendeau, 'Nationalisme et séparatisme', *L'Action nationale*, Vol. XXX, No. 3, March 1955, page 579.

57   24   *Report*, Vol. III, page 294.

34   See Pierre-Elliott Trudeau, *La Grève de l'amiante* (Montreal, 1956), pages 10-37, and his 'Some Obstacles to Democracy in Quebec' in Mason Wade (ed.), *Canadian Dualism*, pages 241-59.

58   6   Maurice Lamontagne, *Le Fédéralisme canadien* (Quebec, 1954).

19   Jean-Marc Leger, 'Aspects of French-Canadian Nationalism', *University of Toronto Quarterly*, Vol. XXVII, No. 3, April 1958, pages 310-29. Hubert Guindon, 'Social Unrest, Social Class and Quebec's Bureaucratic Revolution', *Queen's Quarterly*, Vol. LXXI, No. 2, Summer 1964, pages 150-62.

Page Line

27 *Le Fédéralisme, l'acte de l'Amérique du nord britannique et les Canadiens français*, Mémoire de la Société Saint-Jean-Baptiste de Montréal au Comité Parlementaire de la Constitution du Gouvernement du Québec (Montreal, 1964); *Le Devoir*, August 11, 1964, page 4; Jacques-Yvan Morin, 'The Need for a New Canadian Federation', *Canadian Forum*, Vol. XLIV, No. 521, June 1964, pages 64-6.

60 17 Laurier, 'Le Fédéralisme', page 220.

61 11 Jean-Charles Bonenfant, 'L'Esprit de 1867', *Revue d'histoire de l'Amérique française*, Vol. XVII, No. 1, June 1963, page 38.

QUEBEC AND CONFEDERATION: A LOOK AT SOME
CURRENT PROPOSALS

63 33 Olivar Asselin, 'Sir Wilfrid Laurier', *Pensées françaises* (Montreal, n.d.), pages 101-13.

68 8 Speech to the Canadian Union of Students, September 4, 1964.

14 Jean-Luc Pépin, 'Co-operative Federalism', *Canadian Forum*, Vol. XLIV, No. 527, December 1964, pages 206-10.

70 9 Speech to the Canadian Union of Students, September 3, 1964.

71 9 *Le Fédéralisme* etc., page 118.

12 Jacques-Yvan Morin, 'The Need for a New Canadian Federation', *Canadian Forum*, Vol. XLIV, No. 521, June 1964, pages 64-6. 'Un Nouveau Rôle pour un sénat moribond',

Page Line

           Cité libre, 15th year, No. 68, June-July 1964, pages 3-7.

72   25   *Le Devoir*, September 10, 1964.

      29   Winnipeg *Free Press*, June 19, 1964.

73   6   Michel Brunet, *La Présence anglaise et les Canadiens* (Montreal, 1958), page 292.

      17   Michel Brunet, *Canadians et Canadiens*, page 139.

      29   *Le Fédéralisme* etc., page 107.

75   2   Quebec, 1962.

78   34   *Le Fédéralisme* etc., page 122.

QUEBEC: THE IDEOLOGY OF SURVIVAL

79   19   Brother Jérôme, *Les Insolences du Frère Untel* (Montreal, 1960), pages 55, 67, 83-4.

80   20   Jean-Charles Falardeau, 'The Changing Social Structures', in the work he edited, *Essais sur le Québec contemporain* (Quebec, 1953), page 111.

81   1   Pierre-Elliott Trudeau, 'Some Obstacles to Democracy in Quebec', in Mason Wade (ed.), *Canadian Dualism*, pages 241-9.

82   20   *Le Devoir*, March 7, 1963.

83   1   G. M. Craig (ed.), *Lord Durham's Report* (Toronto, 1963), page 149.

      16   Gustave Lanctot, *Les Canadiens français et leurs voisins du sud* (Montreal, 1941), pages 294-7.

      23   Pierre-Elliott Trudeau, *La Grève de l'amiante*, pages 4-5.

84   11   Léon Dion, 'The Origin and Character of the Nationalism of Growth', *Canadian For-*

Page	Line	
		um, Vol. XLII, No. 516, January 1964, pages 229-33.
	20	H. Manning, *The Revolt of French Canada* (Toronto, 1962).
	26	Albert Faucher and Maurice Lamontagne, 'The History of Industrial Development', in Falardeau (ed.), *Essais sur le Québec contemporain*, page 36.
85	3	Maurice Tremblay, 'Orientation de la pensée sociale', in Falardeau, *op. cit.*, pages 193-208; Pierre-Elliott Trudeau, 'La Province de Québec au moment de la grève', in *La Grève de l'amiante*, pages 1-93; Michel Brunet, 'Trois dominantes de la pensée canadienne-française: l'agriculturisme, l'antiétatisme, et le messianisme', in *La Présence anglaise et les Canadiens*, pages 113-66.
	13	Michel Brunet, *La Présence*, page 119.
	24	Louvigny de Montigny, *Antoine Gérin-Lajoie* (Toronto, 1925), page 72.
	28	H.-R. Casgrain, 'Le Mouvement littéraire au Canada', in *Oeuvres complètes de l'abbé H.-R. Casgrain* (Montreal, 1896), Vol. I, pages 353-75.
	32	Gérard Tougas, *Histoire de la littérature canadienne-française* (Paris, 1960), page 25.
86	7	Edmond de Nevers, *L'Avenir du peuple canadien-français*, page 439.
	20	Robert Rumilly, *Histoire de la Province de Québec* (Montreal, 1943), Vol. X, page 83.
87	2	L.-A. Paquet, 'Sermon sur la vocation de la

Page Line

race française en Amérique', in *Discours et allocutions* (Quebec, 1915), page 187.

23   Louis Hémon, *Maria Chapdelaine* (Paris, 1921), pages 144, 252-3.

88   3   Ringuet (Philippe Panneton), *Thirty Acres* (Toronto, 1960), page 246.

25   Gabrielle Roy, *The Tin Flute* (Toronto, 1959), page 54.

89   3   Dominique Beaudin, 'L'Agriculturisme, margarine de l'histoire', *L'Action nationale*, Vol. XLIX, March 1960, pages 500-30; and, more important, F.-A. Angers, 'Naissance de la pensée économique au Canada-français', *Revue d'histoire de l'Amérique française*, Vol. XV, No. 2, September 1962, pages 204-29.

7   Faucher and Lamontagne, 'The History of Industrial Development', in Falardeau (ed.), *Essais sur le Québec contemporain*, page 28.

90   6   J. Huston (ed.), *Le Répertoire nationale* (Montreal, 1893), Vol. IV, pages 18-19.

25   Albert Faucher, 'La Dualité et l'économique: tendences divergentes et tendences convergentes', in Mason Wade (ed.), *Canadian Dualism*, pages 222-38.

28   John E. Sawyer, 'The Entrepreneur and the Social Order: France and the United States', in William Miller (ed.), *Men in Business* (New York, 1962), page 16.

32   M. Cadieux and P. Tremblay, 'Etienne Parent théoricien de notre nationalisme', *L'Action nationale*, Vol. XIII, 1939, (March) pages 203-19, (April) pages 307-18.

Page	Line	
91	30	André Labarrière-Paulé, *Les Laïques et la presse pédagogique au Canada français au XIXe siècle* (Quebec, 1963), pages 114, 116, 171.
92	6	Faucher and Lamontagne, 'The History of Industrial Development', in Falardeau (ed.), *Essais sur le Québec contemporain*, pages 24-30. For the development of the Quebec economy in the later period, see John Dales, *Hydro-electricity and Industrial Development Quebec 1898-1940* (Cambridge, Mass., 1957).
	28	Errol Bouchette, 'L'Evolution économique dans la Province de Québec', *Proceedings and Transactions of the Royal Society of Canada*, 1901, second series, Vol. VII, pages 119, 122.
93	25	Errol Bouchette, *L'Indépendance économique du Canada français* (3rd edition, Montreal, 1913), pages 30, 188, 198, 200, 270.
	33	*Le Devoir*, July 5, 1963.
94	12	*Ligue Nationaliste Canadienne, Programme*, 1903.
	18	*Le Nationaliste*, June 19, 1904.
95	16	Olivar Asselin, *A Quebec View of Canadian Nationalism* (Montreal, 1909), pages 44, 47, 56.
	25	See Richard Hofstadter, *The Age of Reform* (New York, 1955).
	30	Henri Bourassa, 'The Nationalist Movement in Quebec', *Proceedings of the Canadian*

Page Line

              Club, Toronto, for the Year 1906-7 (Toron-
              to, 1907), pages 56, 58.

96   4   *Le Devoir*, July 19, 1913.

        6   M. K. Oliver, 'The Social and Political Ideas
              of French-Canadian Nationalists', unpub-
              lished Ph.D. Thesis, McGill University,
              1956, chapters 1 and 2.

97   5   Antonio Perrault, 'Enquête sur le national-
              isme', *L'Action française*, Vol. II, February
              1924, page 118.

        7   Michael Oliver, 'Quebec and Canadian De-
              mocracy', *Canadian Journal of Economics
              and Political Science*, Vol. XXIII, No. 4,
              November 1957, pages 504-15.

       14   H. F. Quinn, *The Union Nationale*. See
              especially Appendix B, pages 206-11.

       21   Jean-Marc Leger, 'Aspects of French Cana-
              dian Nationalism', *University of Toronto
              Quarterly*, Vol. XXVII, No. 3, April 1958,
              pages 218-22.

98   4   Gérard Dion and Joseph Pelchat, 'Répenser
              le nationalisme', *L'Action nationale*, Vol.
              XXXI, No. 6, June 1948, pages 402-12.

        7   J. Hulliger, *L'Enseignement social des
              évêques canadiens de 1891 à 1950* (Mont-
              real, 1957). See also the excellent essay by
              Jean-Charles Falardeau, 'Rôle et importance
              de l'Eglise au Canada français', *L'Esprit*,
              Nos. 193-4, August-September 1952, pages
              214-29.

       12   Paul Gérin-Lajoie, *Pourquoi le Bill 60*
              (Montreal, 1963), page 23.

       21   *Le Devoir*, March 7, 1963.

Page	Line	
99	2	Pierre Vadeboncoeur, 'La Ligne du risque', *Situations*, 4th year, Vol. I, page 42.
100	7	Montreal *La Presse*, November 18, 1961.
	9	Pierre Vadeboncoeur, *op. cit.*, page 43; Pierre-Elliott Trudeau, *La Grève de l'amiante, passim.*
	27	Mason Wade, *The French Canadians, 1760-1945* (Toronto, 1955), page 981.
101	6	Fernand Ouellet, *Louis Joseph Papineau. Un Etre divisé* (Ottawa, 1960), page 24.
	23	Pierre-Elliott Trudeau, 'L'Aliénation nationaliste', *Cité libre*, 12th year, No. 33 (new series), March 1961, page 5.
101	33	Jean-Marc Leger, 'Aspects of French Canadian Nationalism', *University of Toronto Quarterly*, Vol. XXVII, No. 3, April 1958, page 323.
102	2	*Le Devoir*, July 5, 1963.
	9	Léon Dion, 'The Origin and Character of the Nationalism of Growth', *Canadian Forum*, Vol. XLII, No. 516, January 1964, page 232.
103	8	Lord Acton, *The History of Freedom and Other Essays* (London, 1922), page 290.

IN THE BOURASSA TRADITION

106	7	Blair Fraser, 'This Is Raymond', *Maclean's Magazine*, January 1, 1944, page 31.
107	19	Henri Bourassa, *Great Britain and Canada* (Montreal, 1902), page 45.
	34	André Laurendeau, 'Le Nationalisme de

Page Line

Bourassa', in *La Pensée de Henri Bourassa* (Montreal, 1954).

108   33   Olivar Asselin, *L'Oeuvre de l'abbé Groulx* (Montreal, 1923), page 90.

110   9   Les Editions du Jour, Montreal, 1962.

114   20   'Manifeste au peuple du Canada', *L'Action nationale*, Vol. XIX, No. 1, January 1942, pages 48-50.

117   29   André Laurendeau, 'Sur une polémique entre Bourassa et Tardivel', *L'Action nationale*, Vol. XLIII, No. 2, February 1954, pages 248-59.

118   18   *A Preliminary Report of the Royal Commission on Bilingualism and Biculturalism* (Ottawa, 1965), page 13.

THE HISTORIAN AND NATIONALISM

119   10   Page Smith, *The Historian and History* (New York, 1964), page 5.

121   26   Abbé Casgrain, 'F.-X. Garneau', *Oeuvres complètes* (Montreal, 1885), Vol. II, page 132.

122   13   Fernand Ouellet, 'Nationalisme canadien-français et laïcisme au XIXe siècle', *Recherches sociographiques*, 1963, Vol. IV, pages 47-70.

124   12   Any of Groulx's casual writings could be used to document this statement. On his near-separatist phase see his essays in *Notre avenir politique* (Montreal, 1923). His later, unenthusiastic acceptance of Confederation may be seen in his essay in *Les Canadiens-*

Page	Line	
		français et la Confédération canadienne (Montreal, 1927).
	18	André Laurendeau, 'Sur une polémique entre Bourassa et Tardivel', *L'Action nationale*, Vol. XLIII, No. 2, February 1954, pages 248-59.
	24	L. Groulx, 'L'Histoire et la vie nationale', *Dix ans d'action française* (Montreal, 1926), page 267.
	27	*Ibid.*, page 269.
	33	*Ibid.*, page 262.
125	18	L. Groulx, 'Si Dollard revenait . . . ', *Dix ans d'action française*, page 122.
126	28	Léon Dion, 'Le Nationalisme pessimiste, sa source, sa signification, sa validité', *Cité libre*, 8th year, No. 20, November 1957, pages 4-11.
127	13	Michel Brunet, *Canadians et Canadiens*, page 45.
	19	Michel Brunet, *La Présence anglaise et les Canadiens*, page 196.
	29	*Le Magazine Maclean*, March 1961, page 57.
128	3	Brunet, *La Présence*, pages 113-66.
	10	André Laurendeau, 'A propos d'une longue illusion', *Le Devoir*, March 19, 1960.
	31	Brunet, *La Présence*, page 145.
129	19	L. Laflèche, *Quelques considérations sur les rapports de la société civile avec la réligion et la famille* (Trois Rivières, 1866), page 73: 'One will be convinced that the Conquest has not been a misfortune for us, but that it has been the providential means which God used to save us as a people.'

Page Line

29   Brunet, *La Présence*, page 112. Here another writer, often criticized by Brunet, expressed a somewhat similar view of the Conquest. See Edmond de Nevers, *L'Avenir du
peuple canadien-français*, page 46. A rather
different explanation for the dominance of
those ideas in French-Canadian thought is
presented in Maurice Tremblay, 'Orientation
de la pensée sociale', in Falardeau (ed.),
Essais sur le Québec contemporain, pages
193-208, and in Pierre-Elliott Trudeau, *La
Grève de l'amiante*, pages 3-90.

130   12   Brunet, *La Présence*, pages 229-30.

21   Jean Hamelin, *Economie et société de la
Nouvelle France* (Quebec, 1961); Fernand
Ouellet, 'Michel Brunet et la problème de la
Conquête', *Bulletin des recherches histori-
ques*, Vol. 62, No. 2, 1956, pages 92-102.

131   9   Brunet, *Canadians et Canadiens*, page 123.

21   *Ibid.*, page 146.

31   *Ibid.*, page 139.

132   22   *La Présence*, page 277.

25   *Ibid.*, page 292.

33   *Canadians et Canadiens*, page 172.

133   10   *Ibid.*, page 165.

13   *La Présence*, page 201.

19   *Canadians et Canadiens*, page 13.

134   4   Brunet, 'The British Conquest: Canadian
Social Scientists and the Fate of the *Cana-
diens*', *Canadian Historical Review*, Vol.
XL, No. 2, June 1959, page 106.

14   Brunet, 'Co-existence Canadian Style',

Page	Line	
		Queen's Quarterly, Vol. LXIII, No. 3, Autumn 1956, page 427.
	22	*La Présence*, page 263.
135	7	*Canadians et Canadiens*, page 30.
	11	*Ibid.*, page 169.
	15	*La Présence*, page 264.
	19	*Ibid.*, page 266.
	28	*Ibid.*, pages 142-6.
136	8	Jean Génest, 'Qu'est-ce que le brunetisme?', *Le Devoir*, April 22, 1961.
	24	*Canadians et Canadiens*, page 39.
138	11	*Ibid.*, page 138.
	33	*Queen's Quarterly*, Vol. LXIII, No. 3, Autumn 1956, page 430.
139	26	*Le Fédéralisme, l'acte de l'Amérique du nord britannique et les Canadiens français*, page 93.
140	18	*Ibid.*, page 96.
141	7	John Higham, 'The Cult of American Consensus: Homogenizing Our History', *Commentary*, Vol. XXVII, 1959, pages 93-101.
	15	Pierre-Elliott Trudeau, *La Grève de l'amiante*.
	33	Pierre-Elliott Trudeau, 'La Nouvelle Trahison des clercs', *Cité libre*, Vol. XIII, No. 46, April 1962, pages 3-16; Albert Breton, 'The Economics of Nationalism', *Journal of Political Economy*, Vol. LXXII, No. 4, August 1964, pages 376-86.
142	14	*Canadians et Canadiens*, page 79.
	22	*Ibid.*, page 44.

THE CANADIAN DILEMMA: LOCKE, ROUSSEAU, OR ACTON?

Page   Line

143   4   F. R. Scott, 'Canada et Canada français',
               L'Esprit, August-September 1952, page 178.

         14   E. P. Taché speaking in the Canadian Assem-
               bly in April 1846.

144   6   André Laurendeau, 'Nationalisme et séparat-
               isme', *L'Action nationale*, Vol. XLIV, No. 7,
               March 1955, page 575.

         26   James Eayrs, 'Sharing a Continent: The
               Hard Issues', in John Sloan Dickey (ed.),
               The United States and Canada (New York,
               1964), page 93.

145   14   Malcolm Ross, *Our Sense of Identity* (To-
               ronto, 1954), page ix.

146   1   G. V. Ferguson, 'The English-Canadian Out-
               look', in Mason Wade (ed.), *Canadian Dual-
               ism*, page 9.

150   13   Henri Bourassa, *La Langue française et
               l'avenir de notre race* (Quebec, 1913), page
               15.

         25   'René Lévesque Speaks of Quebec, National
               State of the French Canadians', originally
               published in *Le Devoir*. Printed in transla-
               tion in F. R. Scott and Michael Oliver, *Que-
               bec States Her Case*, pages 144-5.

151   17   F. H. Underhill, 'Canada and the North At-
               lantic Triangle', in *In Search of Canadian
               Liberalism* (Toronto, 1960), page 257.

152   11   'Mémoire de la Ligue d'Action Nationale à la
               Commission royale d'enquête sur les arts,
               les lettres et les sciences', page 312.

Page	Line	
153	13	Toronto *Globe and Mail*, December 21, 1962.
	24	*Le Devoir*, December 22, 1962. Translated in Scott and Oliver, *Quebec States Her Case*, page 104.
160	2	Peter Gzowski, 'An Open Letter to the French-Canadian Nationalists', *Maclean's* Magazine, October 17, 1964, page 28.
	26	Toronto *Globe and Mail*, September 8, 1964.
161	8	Winnipeg *Free Press*, June 19, 1964; Montreal *Star*, October 1, 1964.
	14	*Le Devoir*, September 10, 1964.
164	3	Jean-Luc Pépin, reported in *Le Devoir*, October 31, 1964.
	20	Maurice Lamontagne, speech to the Club Richelieu de Québec, September 9, 1964; Jean-Luc Pépin, speech to the Institut Canadien des Affaires Publiques, September 12, 1964.
165	7	Speech to the Canadian Club, Montreal, September 28, 1964.
166	5	*Le Devoir*, September 19, 1964.
	24	Pierre-Elliott Trudeau, 'La Nouvelle Trahison des clercs', page 15.
	35	John W. Holmes, 'The Diplomacy of a Middle Power', *The Atlantic*, November 1964, page 106.

THE MEANING OF CONFEDERATION

170	19	Raymond Barbeau, *J'ai choisi l'indépendance* (Montreal, 1961), page 7.

Page	Line	
	25	Raymond Barbeau, *Québec est-il une colonie?* (Montreal, 1962).
	33	Elie Kedourie, *Nationalism*. This book is an indispensable analysis of nationalist ideology.
171	23	*Confederation Debates*, page 45.
172	27	*Ibid.*, page 29.
173	1	Public Archives of Canada, Brown Chamberlin Papers, Macdonald to Chamberlin, February 21, 1856.
	9	*Confederation Debates*, page 44.
	27	*Ibid.*, page 60.
174	28	Public Archives of Canada, New Brunswick, C. O. 189, Gordon to Cardwell, September 22, 1864.
175	4	Sir Robert Herbert (ed.), *Speeches on Canadian Affairs by Henry Howard Molyneux, Fourth Earl of Carnarvon* (London, 1902), pages 10-11. Italics added.
	6	D. G. Creighton, *The Road to Confederation: The Emergence of Canada, 1863-1867* (Toronto, 1964); Thomas Chapais, *Cours d'histoire du Canada* (Quebec, 1934), Vol. VIII, page 162.
	34	Public Archives of Canada, Brown Papers, Brown to Anne Brown, October 27, 1864.
176	7	*Confederation Debates*, page 9.
	21	C. P. Stacey, *Canada and the British Army, 1846-71* (Toronto, 1963), and Robin Winks, *Canada and the United States: The Civil War Years* (Baltimore, 1960).
177	6	*Report of the Royal Commission on Dom-*

Page   Line

inion-Provincial Relations, Book I: *Canada 1867-1939* (Ottawa, 1940), page 29.

18   *Confederation Debates*, page 858.

178   20   *Report of the Royal Commission of Inquiry on Constitutional Problems, Province of Quebec* (Quebec, 1956), Vol. I, page 22.

35   Pierre-Elliott Trudeau, 'Federalism, Nationalism and Reason', in P. A. Crepeau and C. B. Macpherson (eds.), *The Future of Canadian Federalism* (Toronto, 1965), pages 16-35.

180   1   Canada, *House of Commons Debates*, 1886, Vol. I, page 72.

3   John Meisel, *The Canadian General Election of 1957* (Toronto, 1962).

181   9   Eugene Forsey, 'The British North America Act and Biculturalism', *Queen's Quarterly*, Vol. XXXI, No. 2, Summer 1964, pages 141-9.

18   *Confederation Debates*, page 86.

31   Alfred Bernier, *Le Manitoba champs d'immigration* (Ottawa, 1887), page 16.

182   5   Canada, *House of Commons Debates*, 1890, Vol. I, page 546. The speaker was Colonel W. E. O'Brien of 'Noble Thirteen' fame.

10   Fred Landon, 'D'Alton McCarthy and the Politics of the Later Eighties', *Report of the Canadian Historical Association*, 1932, pages 43, 50.

33   Canada, *House of Commons Debates*, 1890, Vol. I, page 745.

183   10   Dom Benoît, *La Vie de monseigneur Taché* (Montreal, 1904), Vol. II, pages 195-6.

Page	Line	
	25	Public Archives of Canada, Laurier Papers, J. S. Willison to Laurier, March 9, 1905.
184	15	*Canadian Annual Review, 1916* (Toronto, 1917), pages 673-4.
	34	Hon. S. J. Latta, in *The Language Question before the Legislative Assembly of Saskatchewan* (Prince Albert, 1919), page 13. The Minister who resigned was the Hon. W. R. Motherwell.
185	17	Public Archives of Canada, Dafoe Papers, Dafoe to Thomas Côté, April 17, 1916.
	27	*Confederation Debates*, page 44. Italics added.
186	11	Dafoe Papers, Henri Bourassa to Dafoe, April 26, 1928.
188	9	Donald Smiley, 'The Two Themes of Canadian Federalism', *Canadian Journal of Economics and Political Science*, Vol. XXXI, February 1965, pages 80-97.
	28	André Laurendeau, 'Y a-t-il une crise du nationalisme?', *L'Action nationale*, Vol. XL, No. 3, December 1952, page 224.
189	6	*Canada français et l'union canadienne*, Société Saint-Jean-Baptiste de Montréal (Montreal, 1954), pages 115-16.
	14	Paul Chamberlain, 'De domination à la liberté', *Parti pris*, Summer 1964.
	31	Claude Ryan, 'The French-Canadian Dilemma', *Foreign Affairs*, Vol. 43, No. 3, April 1965, page 474.

Index